Commendations fo ~~CH00825593~~ s Sea

Chris Russell is one of the best evangelists of our time. ~~He ...~~ he lives – with all the urgency, compassion, and wisdom of one whose life has been transformed by Christ, and who longs for others to know the same love.

To spend time with Chris, whether in person or in the pages of his book, is to be welcomed into and challenged with the reality of the gospel, to learn to 'yearn for the vast and endless sea' of God's unfailing love and to feel encouraged to take our place in God's great story.

Chris Russell introduces us to a world so remarkable we might scarcely believe it to be true, were it not for the witness of true servants of Christ, like Chris, who have made it their home, and the extraordinary power of God to transform, renew, redeem, and restore us.

Read this book and join the many people Chris has guided closer towards the risen Christ, who longs for us to know and love him as he knows and loves us.

Archbishop Justin Welby

One commonly forgotten aspect of Christian belief is excitement. The sheer thrill of it. This book is full of that thrill. It opens all the windows of your house of faith and lets the light stream in. I didn't realise, till I read this book, how musty mine had become.

And speaking of windows, I loved the many allusions, not just to the Bible but to other religious writers, to Van Gogh, to the poet who saw God as the Hound of Heaven, to The Little Prince and many, many more. They operate like a fabulous Advent calendar, each allusion opening a little window that sets you off on another stimulating train of thought.

I finished this book about three days ago and, as you can probably tell, I'm still excited.

Frank Skinner, comedian and TV presenter

Yearning for the Vast and Endless Sea is a gem of a book – inspiring, pastoral, gracious, and every page brims over with Chris Russell's infectious enthusiasm for the gospel. He casts a vision for evangelism that goes far beyond techniques, obligations and clichés and simply brings the reader back to God, back to Jesus and the sheer beauty of the gospel.

Revd Dr Isabelle Hamley, Principal, Ridley Hall, Cambridge

Chris Russell's book is a breath of fresh air, reminding us why the good news is just so utterly good. What I love most is that instead of giving us a 'how-to' manual, Chris takes us right back to the start – inviting us to revisit the wonder, beauty and power of it all. For some this brilliant book will help renew the joy of their salvation. For others it will re-kindle a passion for evangelism. For many it will do both.

Matt Redman, songwriter and worship leader

I may not do God but I am interested in faith, in the Bible, and in those who are genuinely expert about the stories it tells. I have been lucky enough to have had some wonderful conversations with Chris Russell about all of the above and more and am thrilled he has written this book. You do not have to agree with every word to recognise a fine analytical mind, plenty of wisdom, and faith that runs deep and to good effect.

Alastair Campbell

We human beings are creatures who always seek the good. It seems true for all of us. Even when we – or the societies we live in – do very bad things, we're most often motivated by some good, something we think will make life worth living. But we can be very wrong about what is good, tempted to see what is not good as good. This happens to us because the way we access the good is through stories that come to us as a message telling us what is good to live for. In this marvellous book Chris Russell shows us that testifying to the good of the story of Jesus Christ is both the beginning and the end of evangelism. Evangelism is giving narrative shape to the good we encounter by meeting the living Jesus Christ. This is a good book. Chris Russell is a good guide. He gives us a good vision for evangelism. One that is good for the world and good for the church.

Andrew Root, Professor of Youth and Family Ministry, Luther Seminary
and author of the Ministry in a Secular Age series

Chris Russell provides a welcome, at times challenging, but always inspirational reminder of where the pearl is to be found that is the good news of the gospel. The answer at a time of existential crisis for the Church and our world lies in the warming of the heart, clarity of mind and the purposeful delivery that can only be found by making space in ourselves and our institutions for the all-inclusive love of the fisherman who will never throw us back into the sea and the joy-filled and amplified proclamation of his wondrous word.

Lord Paul Boateng, a Vice President of the Bible Society and
Chair of the Archbishops' Council on Racial Justice

In *Yearning for the Vast and Endless Sea*, Chris Russell makes a timely, elegant and impassioned case for Christian evangelism. Fears for the recession of the Church can easily govern its message about Jesus, to the weakening of both. Here instead is a compelling and personal call to be inspired by the Good News itself, and the beautiful landscape offered to all.

Andrew Rumsey, author, songwriter and Bishop of Ramsbury

It is the deepest longing of every soul to know they are loved. Chris Russell captures within this book some of the historic, theological, present beauty of telling the story of love in Jesus through the image of the vast and endless sea. He has encountered grace in a way that widens the vision of the love of God, and lives that generous love in his life and his writing. I commend this book to remind us of the importance of speaking, sharing and inviting others to know the endless love of God found in the person of Jesus Christ.

Canon Sarah Yardley, Mission Lead, Creation Fest UK

Yearning for the Vast and Endless Sea

*The Good News About
the Good News*

Chris Russell

CANTERBURY
PRESS
Norwich

Published in 2024 by Canterbury Press
Editorial office
3rd Floor, Invicta House,
110 Golden Lane,
London EC1Y 0TG, UK

www.canterburypress.co.uk

Canterbury Press is an imprint of Hymns Ancient & Modern Ltd
(a registered charity)

Hymns Ancient & Modern® is a registered trademark of
Hymns Ancient & Modern Ltd
13A Hellesdon Park Road, Norwich,
Norfolk NR6 5DR, UK

British Library Cataloguing in Publication data

A catalogue record for this book is available
from the British Library

ISBN 978-1-78622-517-7

Typeset by Regent Typesetting

Contents

For Leo, Alastair, Paul, Vic, Nathan, Jonny, Brendan,
Alice, Clare, Polly, Steve, Cath, Pete and Jeannie.
Come to the waters …

Introduction

Of course, the assumption of many is that the gospel is not good, and certainly not news. Rather than being 'good' it is suspected of being restrictive and oppressive – and therefore at least unhealthy if not actually harmful.

Instead of being 'news' it is seen as decidedly dated, archaic and belonging to a bygone era that society is glad to see disappear.

But in actual fact, to call the gospel 'good' is the most ludicrous understatement, and as soon as we are able to grasp that, and that its contents are of the most pressing significance, then it *must* be told, or how else will people know it?

And to be utterly focused on this good news – living in grateful response to what we have encountered, and intent that all should have an opportunity to hear this good news – is not just for trendy churches without pews, clergy without collars, extroverts without embarrassment or Christians without nuance, but for every church and all who follow Christ.

Why?

It is not because the church faces near-certain extinction unless we launch a successful recruitment drive.

It is not because we want to maintain a position of influence in a culture that views us as increasingly suspicious and therefore necessary to consign to museums.

It is not because we want to make people like us.

Instead, it is because of the goodness of the good news.

And, like all news, you only know it if you are told.

What evangelism – the spreading of the Christian gospel –

most needs isn't new techniques, courses or heroes. What is needed is a captivating vision of the good news.

Antoine de Saint-Exupéry is best known for writing *The Little Prince*, which for some unimaginable reason continues to be displayed in the children's section of bookshops and libraries. He is credited with having said this:

> If you want to build a ship, don't drum up the people to gather wood, divide the work, and give orders. Instead, teach them to yearn for the vast and endless sea.

Without doubt, there is much to discuss about the 'how to' of evangelism; there is a significant amount to learn about good practice, effective engagement and helpful guidance. But those things aren't the things that come first.

Before anything else, we ourselves need to be grasped by the good news *about* the good news.

All I seek to do here is to take you to the beach, the edge of the ocean, and lift your head so that we all might live in the wonder of the beauty, goodness and truth that we find before us.

Because it's a vast and endless sea.

It is a pearl so exquisite and captivating that, having stumbled across it, we gladly give up everything to make it our own.

It is a hidden treasure that, when we find it, we know we must own, and so we will 'sell everything' to 'buy the field in which it is buried'.

The good news offers us incomprehensible peace, immeasurable joy, and knowledge that is beyond our knowing.

It makes enemies friends, breaks down dividing walls between us and creates the people of the true and living God.

It ...

Too much already? There's more ...

It sets people free and enables them to find this freedom.

It heralds the end of death, the beginning of eternity and the sure and certain hope of everlasting life.

It makes forgiveness possible, it means we are not the worst
thing we have done or the best thing we might achieve.

It means we are not defined or held by our pasts or identified
simply by what we have in the present.

It is the news of transcendent wonder and overwhelming
glory.

For God is for us and not against us.

This love that has come to us will never leave us alone. This
God who came to us has for ever bonded himself to us. There is
nothing that will ever separate us from this love.

Compared to this, all things are rubbish. We would give up
everything for the sake of this good news.

It brings life in its fullness, joy that is the strength of our lives,
and a reason to be.

It declares and guarantees that one day all things will be made
new; that justice will flow like mighty unstoppable streams and
the arc of history does, in fact, bend towards truth.

In the presence of the gospel, racism, sexism, classism, xeno-
phobia, homophobia and every form of prejudice are unmasked
and declared to be godless. All are welcome, everyone is invited,
no one is left outside.

For God has done what we could not do.

And this news must be shared.

There is an ancient story of the siege of the town of Samaria.
The enemy had surrounded these poor people and laid siege to
their homes. The situation inside the town was catastrophic.
All seemed lost. Outside the town, at the gates, four lepers
decided to risk going to the enemy camp and pleading for their
lives. When they arrived, they discovered the reality was completely different from what they expected. The tents, which
they thought contained the ultimate threat to all of their lives,
were empty of people and full of everything they needed or
could hope for. God had acted to save them and the enemy
had scarpered. Immediately they started to plunder the tents
and stockpile the treasure – until one turned to their friends

and said, 'What we are doing is not right. This is a day of good news, we cannot keep it to ourselves.'

For too long the church and we Christians have kept everything to ourselves that has fallen into our laps because of God's saving work in Christ. We have hoarded the treasure.

My contention is that in, through and because of Jesus, everything has changed. For everyone. This gift is only ours because we are those who have had our eyes, ears, hands and hearts opened so we can say 'yes' to all that is ours from God in Christ.

The truth is that God has acted to change everything for everyone in Jesus Christ. Yet the majority of people live, or maybe just exist, in terrible ignorance of what has been done for them, what they are invited into and what they can be part of.

Evangelism is simply the refusal to keep this good news to ourselves.

In the following pages we will explore the *What, How, Who, When, Where* and *Why* of the gospel.

And because I am persuaded that this all-encompassing belief is needed to begin to do justice to all that is ours in the good news, we have to hold the tension between things that are too often collapsed into one thing – especially in a culture that seems to regard binaries in Christianity as the best place to set up camp. Each chapter will contend that two positions – which have at times been disastrously divided – must be kept together.

Chapter 1 asks, 'What is the gospel?' The gospel isn't a slogan, a statement or a doctrine, but the actual and particular person Jesus Christ. So in fact the good news is *not* a 'What?' but a 'Who?'. Because Jesus is inseparable from the kingdom he comes to declare, establish and rule, to encounter the gospel is to experience the kingdom. To do justice to what the gospel is, we have to hold the primacy of the person of Christ in the one hand and the primacy of the kingdom in the other. We hold in tension Jesus and the kingdom he inaugurated.

Chapter 2 explores *How* the gospel is shared or communicated. Unashamedly it is held that essential to the gospel is its telling; it must be *proclaimed*. Words are integral to the announcement – for it can only be known if it is told. But because essential to the core of the message is news of the Word made flesh, we only comprehend these words when they take flesh and we encounter them *lived*. To fully and adequately proclaim the gospel we need to engage our mouths and ears, and also show what these words mean with our hands and our feet. This holds in tension our words and our actions.

Chapter 3 considers *Who* bears the gospel? Beginning with the recognition that we rely upon the primacy of God's work as Father, Son and Holy Spirit to redeem the world, this God is the content of the good news and its enabler – the great missionary evangelist. But because of how God is in and for the world, we find ourselves co-opted as God's agents of the realization of redemption. This is humanity in partnership. This should cause us to stand in awe of the God who makes all the moves, and yet find ourselves employed as God's co-workers. Essentially this holds in tension God's agency and human agency.

In Chapter 4, the question is *When* does the gospel take effect? There are moments to hold out for and celebrate that change everything – moments that define and set a new way, moments of conversion and decision. But the gospel journey is a long obedience in the same direction, which takes the whole road – and more – for it to have its transforming effect on us. The only way to take time seriously is by holding out moments and seasons – enabling us to fulfil a vocation to teach the world how to tell the time. The tension to hold to is between moments of conversion and the process of the journey of faith.

Chapter 5 explores *Where* does the gospel come to us? On the one hand, the gospel meets the deepest desires of the core of our being and yet we encounter it as news that comes from outside and apart from us. The gospel gives rest to our restless hearts – in it our deepest and most personal longings are realized. Yet it also comes to us from *outside* of us, addressing us and calling us to account. The tension to maintain is the relationship between internal resonances and external revelation.

Chapter 6 asks *Who* is the gospel for? Because of the enormity of God's love, and his will for us, in Christ the guest list is all-inclusive. The gospel is for all of us – every person is called individually. God's desire is that all should receive the benefits of Christ. But this is nothing like individualism, because each person is called to find themselves as created and sent out on behalf of the world. The vital tension to maintain is between the personal and the universal – every person and all people.

The question for Chapter 7, the final chapter, is *Why* evangelism? For what reason do we proclaim the good news? The answer is, we do it for God's sake and for the way the gospel works within us for the whole world. The gospel is the priority of the church *because* of God, and our being called to be where Jesus is. This gospel takes effect in and through the church – in itself this calls for profound renewal and reform. But it also re-creates the world and sets things on a scale that is impossible to grasp or overstate. We are being held in tension by God and the world.

To adequately answer each question we must hold two equally firm commitments in each hand – of course, each commitment pulls us; it might feel simpler if we could just 'collapse' this tension, but we must hold on to it. Holding in each hand two things that pull is not always comfortable or easy. In fact, it means we have to maintain a cruciform position. I am convinced it is the posture of Christ to the world he came to save.

I believe we must do this now. Our predecessors cannot do our work for us; we ourselves need to inhabit the world of the gospel.

Everything that follows is a distillation of all I have come to hold dear as a follower of Jesus Christ, and particularly what I have learned through the honour of serving as Archbishop Justin's Adviser on Evangelism and Witness. The most shaping experience of my life has been the privilege of being part of St Laurence, Reading, for 19 years. As a church we learned to live together as if the good news is actually true – and found that it is. I am so grateful to all of God's people at St Laurence, whose exceptional quality and commitment I can't find words for – especially the young people whose lives have shown me the transforming power of the gospel. My thanks go to companions in conversations about the good news: Craig and Emma, Christian, Stephen, Dan, Pete, Anthonia, Frank, Andy Root, Ula, Amy, J John, Martyn and Emily, colleagues here at Lambeth, and all the Youthscapers. Also, to those who so kindly took the time to read these words – Andrew Rumsey, Stephen Hance, Hannah Steele, Richard Sudworth and Annette Smith; I am more grateful to you than I can say.

Love beyond telling goes to my girls – Belinda, Hopey, Jessie and Dora. You mean everything to me. And especially to Belinda, who lives oblivious of the beauty and power of her witness and effect – you have done more to shape my thinking and acting than anyone. I know that I don't want to know who I am without you.

For us as a family, these last few months, the sun has been eclipsed as we have journeyed through the valley of the shadow of death, as our 12-year-old nephew, Jack, was plagued by a rare and ruinous cancer. This vale of tears has been mysterious and devastating, and the anticipation of death has been brutal, cruel and crushing. Yet, yet, yet ... We know the presence of the one who was dead but is now alive, who has overcome the foe of death and who lives to welcome Jack personally to the vast and endless sea of eternal life.

The dedication is to those friends who probably wouldn't call themselves Christians, and so wouldn't pick up a book such as this. I will keep praying daily that you come to the waters: Leo, Alastair, Paul, Vic, Nathan, Jonny, Brendan, Alice, Clare, Polly, Steve, Cath, Pete and Jeannie. My sincere hope is that I have done something to open up the curtains on the wonder of the good news. The goodness of this good news is a thing of which I am completely and utterly persuaded. Of course, there are things that I struggle with and things I am probably wrong about. But my real fear is, when it comes to talking about God and how good God's good news is, I have not nearly begun to sing adequate praise.

I

What is the Gospel?

The *what* of the gospel

It's a really poor start. Because the title of the first chapter – what is the Gospel? – sets us off in the wrong direction. But it does help us to define some basic terms.

'Gospel' is a key word in the Bible; it comes from the Greek words *euaggelion/euangelion*. But it's not just a biblical word; it was also an everyday word. Some of those who wrote our scriptures could only do justice to the revolutionary thing they were bearing witness to by making up a brand-new word. However, more often than not, they took a normal everyday word and co-opted it for God. 'Gospel' is one of these words. It was used throughout the world to describe the communication of something that was both too good and too important not to be made known. The word literally breaks down like this:

eu = good
angelios = message/announcement/news

In the Hebrew Bible it's a message people bring, carry, run with and rush to tell. And always because something has happened that changes everything, which is of such consequence that people need to know. And also because the only way we find out things is by people telling us. It's news that we want to know.

Like cold water to a thirsty soul, so is good news from a far country. (Proverbs 25.25)

'Gospel' is a word that describes what it does: good news is announced.

But what is this news that is being announced?

At this point some introduce the gospel as an 'object' – a 'thing' that can be put into our hands. A defined, expertly honed, tightly specified and articulated set of words, something that can be conveyed like a static formula. It is almost as if, in a few quickly dispensed sentences, 'the gospel' can be completely summed up. Of course, I am not saying that in some settings the truth of the gospel can't be, or shouldn't be, described simply and concisely, with pictures, images, words and memorable phrases. But surely everything that needs to be expressed about the gospel cannot be conveyed in a prepared formula of doctrinal statements or using some carefully crafted sentences. Evangelism is not the 'dispensing' of the gospel – it is not a product that simply needs to be 'applied'.

This is *not* because the gospel cannot be defined, and it's not because we don't have the right words. The gospel is distinct and unique, but it is *not* an object, a formula, a 'thing' that we can learn by heart, so that in the right situation we can simply pull a cord on our backs and recite it to anyone and everyone. The gospel is not a commodity, or brand, a cut-and-pasted block of statements, a moral code, a product to be dispensed in a sealed packet to which we just need to add water.

The gospel is not a *What*, it's a *Who*. The gospel is a person:

The beginning of the gospel of Jesus Christ ... (Mark 1.1)

I have fully proclaimed the good news of Christ. (Romans 15.19)

When I came to Troas to proclaim the good news of Christ ... (2 Corinthians 2.12)

... we were the first to come all the way to you with the good news of Christ. (2 Corinthians 10.14)

This *Who* is a particular, unique, specific person: Jesus of Nazareth, the Christ of God, the son of Mary; it is not a set of statements, facts, doctrines, dogmas, beliefs or even truths. It *can* be conveyed in these ways, and attempts can be made to clearly and accurately describe the content that is the good news. But that content will never be able to do full justice to the nature of the good news, because the good news is one – Jesus – who stands before us as a living person. He is the one before whom we take up an appropriate position – standing in attentiveness/kneeling in reverence/lying prostrate in awe; we are in the presence of this person who is himself the definition of the good news. Pope Francis insists, 'We should not think the gospel message must always be communicated by fixed formulations learned by heart or specific words which express an invariable content.'[1] Instead, to encounter the gospel is to meet with a person – Jesus Christ.

The *Who* of the gospel

All of Christianity is a response to the person and event of Jesus Christ.

This means that as we consider the gospel we enter an encounter.

Of course, we approach faith with all sorts of questions. These are questions that we ask of everything, testing its value, its validity and its veracity. The German theologian and martyr Dietrich Bonhoeffer was adamant that when we consider Jesus Christ we are not engaging with an idea, a belief or a schema. We are engaging with a person. Bonhoeffer insists that the most significant of questions is, 'Who is it that I confront when I look at Jesus?' This *Who* question quickly gets reflected back on us, as Jesus continually did in his earthly life. He asks us who we are, what we are seeking, and if we will leave everything behind to follow him. To encounter who this Jesus is transforms us.

Jesus is not just communicating a message or bringing a piece of information. He is not an authorized spokesman for some other person. He does not remind us of what we have forgotten or the things we really should have picked up already in life, but were asleep at the back of the class. He is what he teaches. He himself creates the conditions for us to know him. He is his own authority. He is the good news – in all he is; in all that he does; in all that he says; in all that he achieves; in all that he lives for, suffers for, dies for, is raised for; in all that happens to him; in all he chooses to do and all that was done to him; in all that he continues to be and do; in what is promised and what is yet to come to pass.

In an attempt to give my daughters some kind of cultural education I have dragged them off to various galleries. My favourites are either ones displaying Caravaggios or the Tate Modern. They placate me on the first (just about!) but pour scorn with their 'That looks like something I did in Year 2' contempt on the second. A couple of years ago there was a fascinating piece on the third floor; it was a large hanging sphere that you could walk around and that was open on one side so you could look in. When you looked in you couldn't see any beginning or end, any edges or boundaries; the thing you were looking into seemed to have no bottom, no top, no sides, no limits – except when you stepped back and walked around it. When you stared into it, it was mesmerizing and felt as if you were staring into eternity. In introducing Jesus, St John says in his epistle, 'We declare to you what was from the beginning, what we have heard, what we have seen with our eyes, what we have looked at and touched with our hands' (1 John 1.1). Jesus of Nazareth is a particular person who can be walked around, taking up a distinct space. Yet within him is more than we can ever comprehend. With Jesus Christ we are saying as much as is possible to say about a human being. If we were to attempt to say everything about him and what he has done, then – as it says in John's Gospel – 'I suppose that the world itself could not contain the books that would be written' (John 21.25).

4

The good news is about this particular person, with this particular history; and apart from Jesus, Christianity has no universal message to tell. The eyewitness accounts of Jesus, written for the sake of those who weren't his contemporaries, are themselves called Gospels, because they unashamedly relate the good news that is Jesus of Nazareth. He is good news because of all he is and all he does. It is impossible to say or capture adequately all that this is or all that he does. But he is proclaimed as the *content* of the good news – it is what God has done and continues to do, in, through, by and for the sake of Jesus Christ.

The significance of this can only be adequately grasped as we consider Jesus in context – as the fulfilment of promises to his ancestors, as the realization of all that had been held out and hoped for, as the one who was speaking to these people, in this place, at this specific moment in their political, social and economic history. The good news is told by telling the story of Jesus. And while this good news took place in a historical context, the response it generates now isn't merely or primarily an assimilation of facts or details. It's a story that involves us. We are players, participating in what the story reveals. Or, rather, participating with Jesus – the one the story reveals.

Everything about Jesus is everything about God.

To tell the history of Jesus is to narrate the true story of God.

Jesus shows us who God is

So in presenting the gospel we are always presenting a person – one with a distinct story and history in a specific time and place. But it is not just the tale of a bygone hero or tales from yesteryear. This is because this Jesus is alive and living and encountered today; and in the one he is, the one he was and the one he will be (Hebrews 13.8), there is an utter certainty to the good news. It is entirely 'weight-bearing'.

If the gospel is a person, then evangelism is an invitation to meet this person. It is an introduction and compelling

5

encouragement to listen to Jesus, paying attention to what he does, responding to his questions, finding ourselves in his presence and coming to love and serve him. It is to understand life as lived in the light of this person.

This encounter with Jesus is a whole-of-life-impacting experience. This isn't faith as an app on our pre-existing operating system – it's not an addition to life. (As if what we need is another 'thing' in our lives!) Faith isn't just one item that has been missing, like an absent plank in our fence, that Jesus can patch.[2]

Sometimes we embark on evangelism as if it were some kind of marketing strategy; in other words, as if there is a product (the gospel) that *we* have and *others* need. To persuade them that they need it, we may show, like any good advertiser, what their life is missing without it; what the benefits are to them in taking up the offer. So we employ the most persuasive and successful techniques for securing a sell. In some ways we can't help but do this – we live in a consumer age where everything life is about, everything that makes life meaningful, can be acquired and possessed. We select and organize our own worlds to our own tastes, with our own needs and requirements as the defining rationale for our choices. There are billions of pounds spent in shaping our desires every hour of every day. In such a world evangelism sometimes appears to have seamlessly slid on to a stall at the market place. In such surroundings the gospel is pitched as an offer for the Life You Always Wanted, the Good Life, the Authentic Life, the Happy Life – and Jesus is the means by which you get everything you were always missing.[3]

But what if what we think we want isn't actually what we need?

What if what we need, above everything else, isn't more things, more stuff, but a relationship, a living connection, with our creator and judge, our beginning and our end?

The Jewish philosopher Martin Buber brought clarity around our essential existence as persons in the world characterized not by 'I – It' but by 'I – Thou'. He said if we fall into the habit of relating to one another as things, rather than as another *person*, we are goners. This is rooted in our creation and formation as those made in God's image, who are called to relate to God not as an 'It' but as a 'Thou'. If the divine is an impersonal 'It' the centre of everything is impersonal. However, the revelation of God in Christ has led Christians to be most sure of this truth about God: God is Father, Son and Holy Spirit; being-in-relationship. And at the very least this means at the heart of everything created and uncreated is the divine being who isn't an 'It', an impersonal thing, but three-in-one, pure love. And if God is personal, mutual and generous relationship is at the heart of everything that is. If God were a 'thing', our interacting with him would be some kind of scheme for getting something for ourselves. In such a system, we are in control, we are in the driving seat. And it's all about us. However, if the gospel is a person, this Jesus 'in whom are hidden all the treasures of wisdom and knowledge' (Colossians 2.3), then to be presented with the gospel is to stand before one whose reality defines everything else that is.

This Jesus invites, questions, calls, challenges, demands, insists and reveals what is only possible by him and through him. The reality this one proclaims is himself. The offer of the gospel is himself. In Jesus we learn as true what before we could only guess at: who God is and how God is for us. Here is loving-kindness, mercy, grace, understanding, judgement, patience, faithfulness, commitment, sacrificial love and solidarity, rescue and redemption, salvation and a thousand new starts. And we are invited to know these not as statements and principles – but as the way God is with us. We are met with one who embodies the nature, character and personhood of God and what that God desires for us. In fact, to describe as 'good news' the revelation of who God truly is, how he relentlessly loves us and what he has irreversibly done to save the world might seem rather an understatement.

It is astounding and moving beyond words.

We must summon up all beauty and joy, wisdom and energy to seek to begin to express the height, breadth and depth of it. Such response is called worship.

Evangelism is pulling the curtain back and inviting people into an encounter with Jesus Christ, opening the space up so people can hear his words for themselves, can sense his love in their hearts, his challenge in their choices, can comprehend his actions as being for them. All-involving, all-consuming, all-encompassing, all-freeing. And because he is alive and loving he lives to draw people into this transforming meeting. Evangelism is an introduction to the person of Jesus Christ.

Jesus shows us who we are

The good news of Jesus Christ isn't simply about who God is, but who we are.

The good news is about who we are, who we might be, who we can be, who we must be, who we surely will be; we are 'in Christ' – it is a phrase that is used repeatedly and dramatically, dozens more times than the word 'Christian' in the New Testament. To 'be found in him' (Philippians 3.9) describes the driving intention behind the work of God in Jesus Christ.[4] There is an urgency to this, an almost don't-live-for-a-moment-longer apart from this reality. Wake up! Turn around! Do not delay! See who God is and what this God has done for you and his whole world in Christ and make it your reason for living.

This reality has been made possible and actual by the life, death and resurrection of Jesus Christ. Jesus does not simply offer me a different take on the world or give me new perspectives for seeing myself, others, the world and God. I am not given new lenses, fresh understandings or unusual viewpoints. It is not an unusual jar of spice to just add to the normal dish of life. No, the good news in this Jesus is the announcement of events that have brought change and alteration, difference for everyone and everything. As St Irenaeus says, 'By his coming Christ brought with him all newness!' It is of what has happened, what has been achieved, what has been made possible, because of what has actually taken place. And what has come to pass is reconciliation.

Jesus is God's ultimate commitment to the world that God created. God making known God's nature, God's character and God's will, revealing the truth of all that God is and all that we are. And God does this by and in and through Jesus. He reveals what is true about God and what is true about humanity. This is done not through declarations or pronouncements, but through events that change reality and make a new actuality possible – because, in reality, a mere declaration changes nothing.

What we learn by this, what we receive because of this, what we experience in this, is good, good news. What we learn is beyond our wildest dreams. It is better than we could ever have hoped for. It is (almost) too good to be true.

For we learn that we are of immeasurable worth to God; that God counts us to be of such value – such is his affection and desire for us, such is the divine one's commitment and allegiance to us – that God would not be without us or apart from us. God goes to every length possible to reveal to us that he is our God. The God who is for us and with us. The God who, while having no need of us, will spend his greatest delight to win our presence and companionship. God does this not simply by words, but by freely and even joyfully choosing to show us the full extent of his love by suffering alongside of us, because of us – and ultimately dying for us. In this death God chooses to be for all people, embarking on the most inclusive action of all time; to draw all people to himself. There is no other act that can convey a stronger, more committed, more resolute and sure 'yes' to us – every single one of us – than the life and death of this Jesus. However, the 'yes' also contains a 'no', for we are not what we would be, or hope to be. We are not all we present ourselves to be.

On BBC Radio 4 the other day, at 7.45 a.m. a contributor on *Thought for the Day* shared her conviction that 'people are inherently good'. She was reflecting on the sacrifice of Folajimi Olubunmi-Adewole, an astonishing 20-year-old young man who died after jumping off a London bridge into the water to save a drowning woman. We are, of course, right to stand in awe of such sacrifice. It shows something beautiful about our humanity, but there is more to be said.

Just 11 minutes earlier, at 7.34 a.m. on the same day, on the same radio programme, a woman called Zoe Dronfield was interviewed. For many months of her life she had been subjected to unspeakable violence by an ex-partner who had stalked her, assaulted her, abused her, raped her, stabbed her and attacked her. She had been hospitalized for a very long time. Her attacker had done this before to other women.

To put those two contributions next to each other is too much. The temptation is to make both exceptions. Exceptional bravery and heroism against exceptional cruelty and abuse. Extraordinary goodness in one corner and utter depravity in the other. However, as each of us face Jesus Christ, we are confronted by the news that we are simultaneously good and bad, capable of immense kindness and devastating wickedness. It is what the German theologian Martin Luther termed *simul creatus et peccator* – humans are simultaneously sinners *and* made in the image of God.[5]

Jesus Christ is the one who not only shows us this, but the one who enters into this condition in order to save us from it. We truly see our humanity laid bare in Jesus – what happened to him as he was betrayed, captured, unjustly tried, falsely accused, tortured and murdered is what we do to one another but, worse still, what we do to God.

During the Covid-19 pandemic at its most deadly, we faced the fact that we were a mortal danger to one another; it was quite possible we could infect another with a deadly virus. As stark as this time was, the truth is that we, all of us and each of us, have already caught a deadly virus that we can pass on through everything we do and say, think and create. In and of ourselves we are incurably lost and infectious. The human race is desperately turned in on itself and this has a devastating effect and impact. We can't be vaccinated against it – even though society seems to have naively assumed it isn't pernicious. We cannot cure ourselves. The healing we need cannot come from ourselves, for we are all similarly and fatally 'infected'. Sin is an infectious disease. As Fleming Rutledge says in her wonderful book *The Crucifixion*, 'From beginning to end, the Holy Scriptures testify that the predicament of fallen humanity is so serious, so grave, so irremediable from within, that nothing short of divine intervention can rectify it.'[6]

The good news is that, in Jesus Christ, God has done what we could not do. A saviour has come for our healing. In him we are not simply diagnosed, but healed. This change happens not because we are confronted with uncomfortable information about ourselves, but through the one who becomes what we are, so we might become what he is. Jesus of Nazareth – the only human not infected with the deadly virus of sin – immerses himself in this world where everyone else is a carrier and contaminator. He comes without protective gear and doesn't keep his distance. In fact, the very reason he comes is not simply to diagnose, but to save. He can only do this, though, by freely taking all that we cannot help but carry.

Come then to the ridge at the top of a gorge above the River Jordan sometime around AD 30. There are crowds gathered to see the action. It's all happening in the river itself. A strangely charismatic figure – who of course we now know as John the Baptist – takes time from denouncing those watching, to plunge the next person in the queue into the water of the Jordan. His message is simple: 'Repent'. Change. Turn. Stop going that way. Why is he saying this? What's the rush? God is coming back to his people, so you'd better be ready. And in order to be ready you need to come on to God's side from your side; to admit you are not living as you are supposed to live and decide to make a change.

The sign that someone was on board for this was being plunged in the water, as if they were drowning what they *had* been, so they could start again. John called it baptism.

It's quite a spectacle, which is why so many have taken a

position on the ridge watching the steady stream of those who are repenting. Each one represents a confession. Each one is declaring themselves to be in need of change. Joining the back of the queue you notice a man who you knew from the northern village you grew up in – Joseph and Mary's son, Jesus. You catch yourself being surprised by him joining in with this – he never seemed to be one of the bad ones. You wonder what he is repenting of …

Of course, he doesn't say or explain himself. He goes down into the water and comes back out. As he comes up for air there is a distinct change in the atmosphere, which seemed to be heralded by a bird swooping down on him. Everyone catches their breath and wonders what they have just witnessed. But then he leaves the river and walks away into the desert. And you think – there is just another sinner repenting. Of course you do.

Verse 5.21 in 2 Corinthians claims, 'For our sake God made him to be sin who knew no sin, so that in him we might become the righteousness of God.'

Jesus the sinner. I know, I know … the whole faith is built on the fact that Jesus was able to carry our sin because he did *not* carry his own; he was able to be judged in our place because he had no judgement to face. But it is my belief that from the moment Jesus comes out of the waters of baptism he starts to bear a burden he didn't have when he entered the waters. He begins to carry the sins of the world. Because here he is now, counted among the sinners. He absorbs everything that is wrong, everything that is bad, all that is evil and all that is wicked. He bears it not just on his shoulders, but in his person. And he defeats it by allowing it to do its worst to him. Because he is not carrying his own sin he is able to open his hands to receive the nails of ours.

Jesus' life and death confronts us with devastating information about ourselves: that we are sinners. We are not asked if we *want* to be such people; the question is whether we are ready to be told by Christ that we are. Jesus doesn't simply die *for* us but *because* of us.

This means that while we are drawn to explain the cross of Jesus as God's solidarity with us – Jesus as the co-sufferer – we must also talk of the fact that Jesus suffers because of us. We are those who crucified him. The cross is not the story of our innocence and inherent goodness; instead, it's proof of our corrupted nature, which means we make choices for ourselves to the fatal detriment of others – and God.

This means that the *Who* of the gospel confronts each of us with a stark choice, one that we are never quite ready for – we either choose ourselves or Jesus. Dietrich Bonhoeffer put it even more harshly, 'When a human being confronts Jesus, the human being must either die or kill Jesus.'[7]

But Jesus has already been killed. So the only true and wise response is to say 'yes' to all that he has done and to live openly and gladly having been given his gifts of grace. This will of course require us to turn away from living for ourselves. That's called repentance, and it has the closest possible proximity and relationship to receiving the grace offered to all sinners, not just once, but continually.

The offer is that in recognizing who this Jesus is and what he has done, we find ourselves in an entirely different place than we were when without him. In fact, we find ourselves in a whole new reality. We are not ever without him, apart from him, for we are 'in Christ'.

Moreover, what has been achieved in Christ creates a new people. The walls that divide are taken down, and a new way of living and being together isn't just made possible, but made actual.

Faith is to enter into all that Christ has done for us. The way in is always the same – it's the entry point that he himself is always positioned at, waiting for us: 'Christ Jesus, who, though he was in the form of God, did not consider equality with God something to be exploited, but emptied himself' (Philippians 2.5–7). This 'emptying himself' is a stunning theme in Jesus. The Greek word for it is *kenosis* – it's a laying aside, casting off, choosing one thing and not another. *Kenosis* is a word with consequences – and those consequences for Jesus are stooping low and encountering us in the depths. This meeting us is where opposites collide and yet are 'married': divine/human, life/suffering, strength/weakness, righteous/cursed, sinner/*imago Dei*. God does this because this is what he is like – his love always takes the form of the cross. And so the only place that any of us enter into Christ is in those same depths of self-emptying.

There is something that is utterly elemental about the good news – it is to respond to the God who stands before us in Jesus Christ, the one who was and who is and who is to come. Of course, you can never adequately comprehend the scope of the gospel. But it is when we consider that this *Who* comes not to have books written about him, but to transform the world, that we face into the utter complexity and enormity of the good news.

Jesus Christ comes to rule the world. And when God rules the world you won't believe the change.

The kingdom of God

Jesus' first public words are evangelizing ones – 'The time is fulfilled, and the kingdom of God has come near; repent, and believe in the good news' (Mark 1.15).

This gospel would have been like fresh water on parched land to people who had been waiting for their God to come to them as King. They had known kings before, and knew the impact of bad and corrupt ones and the difference brought by holy and righteous ones. But the king they really wanted to rule over them was God. When God returned to his people to reign, they believed everything would change. All wrongs would be righted, all injustices would be dealt with, all suffering would end and all sadness would be turned to joy. The old age characterized by sin and suffering, by foreign rulers and oppressive threat, would be no more, and all they had ever longed for would be reality. No wonder the cry in Isaiah goes up, 'O that you would tear open the heavens and come down' (Isaiah 64.1).

With such anticipation, imagine the reaction Jesus received when he stood up and read the ancient prophecy within these chapters of promise and hope in Isaiah, about the longed-for return and reign of Yahweh:

The Spirit of the Lord is upon me,
because he has anointed me to bring good news to the poor.
He has sent me to proclaim release to the captives and recovery of sight to the blind,
to let the oppressed go free, to proclaim the year of the Lord's favour.
(Luke 4.18–19)

The good news is not simply that God has come to rule the world, but that because of who he is and how he does it, everything we have longed for has begun.

Jesus' life is evidence of what life in the kingdom is like – hungry people are fed with more food than they need; an abundance of fine wine is produced; those who are blind can see; those who have been chained up because they were a threat to themselves and others are freed and healed; those unable to walk can jump for joy; those who have swindled neighbours out of money freely give it back. The scope of the kingdom couldn't be bigger – it's a tree that all the birds of the air come to nest in; it begins as the tiniest seed but grows into the biggest of trees.

The good news that is ours, and the whole world's, is that, in Jesus, God has come to reign. It is a *coup d'état* – a God take-over, a dismantling of what was and a seizing back of what is rightfully God's. It is not universally welcomed, applauded or joined in with. In fact, those who have the most to lose are in outright hostility to it. The evil it comes to bind and eliminate launches a ferocious attack to destroy its King – not realizing that his willing acquiescence to this death is, in fact, his means of victory and the guarantee of evil's most certain defeat.

The lamb of God takes away the sin of the world. Previously, we noted that in the way individuals treat Jesus we see evidence of what persons do to God, but in the systems that try to destroy the Son of God we see the war of the kingdoms. As the – allegedly – most powerful political figure, Pilate, and what the whole Roman Empire stands for, meets Jesus in the last 24 hours of his life we notice how Jesus, the one without any trappings of power of symbols of authority, is actually the one doing the calling to account, the judging, the sentencing and the proclamation of a new more powerful kingdom. Jesus is seen as a direct threat to every system of government and authority, and rightly so. But God isn't simply a threat. God is the victor.

The good news is that in Jesus' birth, life, death, resurrection and ascension, God's reign has begun. There is no sense anywhere in scripture that what God is primarily concerned about is our internal lives, our religious practices, our 'spiritual' outlook. In the Acts of the Apostles again and again the first Christians are thrown in prison because of the threat they are to the political status quo. Note the accusation against them in Beroea:

> 'These people who have been turning the world upside down have come here also ... They are all acting contrary to the decrees of the emperor, saying that there is another king named Jesus.' The people and the city officials were disturbed when they heard this ... (Acts 17.6–8)

Of course they were disturbed, because the kingdom challenges every other pretender to thrones, power and authority. And we know that the history of our humanity is the history of certain people 'running the show' for their own ends – always at the expense of those they think are worth less. Such people acquire power to ensure they can live like gods.

With Jesus, the end of all monopolies of control and domination at the expense of God's children is promised. I hang my Western head in shame at the collaborations with evil powers that we have made, and built our society upon. What plagues racism, misogyny, secular capitalism, privilege, homophobia

and violence have wreaked (and continue to wreak) upon humanity and the whole of creation. And of course the church of Jesus
Christ has given cover, advocacy and legitimacy to such princi-
palities and powers; and disgracefully we still do.

But the kingdom of God is an end to all oppression and
tyranny. Of course, if you have done your best to acquire
everything now, you might think you don't have any need. If
you are someone who has most to lose you might end up fight-
ing to maintain what you think you have a right to. For many,
the reality of the kingdom of God is bad news, but only because
they are held in the thrall of systems that are idolatrous and evil.
That's why if you have nothing, or find yourself at the bottom,
if you are always left outside or rejected, if you are powerless or
overlooked – it's so much easier to see this good news.

The kingdom of God strikes no power deals and doesn't
enter into coalitions. There is no throne-sharing or succession
planning. Jesus is King and his trappings of power are only
those things that speak of his radical rule of love – the crown
is one of thorns; the throne is a cross made of wood. The raw
power is love.

We live in expectation and anticipation of this. It is not yet
fully realized, but it's future culmination is certain. Its coverage
and expansion is entirely a result of the continuing ministry of
Jesus, which he exercises by the Holy Spirit primarily through
his body, the church. The establishment of the kingdom can
only be built as we follow Jesus' ways of humility, subversion,
companionship, hospitality, acceptance, mercy, challenge,
rebellion, sacrifice – and love, love, love. Outposts of the kingdom are most apparent among those whom Jesus has always
chosen to spend his time with – the poor, the marginalized and
those who have no hope apart from God.

Signs of this kingdom are everywhere, and not only in those
who know the King. The good news names Jesus as the ground
of all beauty, truth and goodness. All beauty is his beauty, all
truth is his truth, all goodness is his goodness. At this point my
friend Leo is vigorously protesting 'You can't do that', and it

is worth just exhaling and weighing the enormity of this assertion. What? Claiming everything for this Jesus? Yes. It gets no bigger than this. For he is the one in whom 'all things in heaven and on earth were created, things visible and invisible ... all things have been created through him and for him. He himself is before all things, and in him all things hold together' (Colossians 1.16–18). This is the goodness of the kingdom of the one who is logos and wisdom, temple and tabernacle, truth and life, promise and guarantee, Messiah and Saviour, Son of God and Son of Man, Jesus of Nazareth and Jesus the Christ. To proclaim the reality of the kingdom is to acknowledge that Jesus is the servant King, at work through his Spirit to bring the benefits of his rule to all people, in all times, in all places.

Of course, this kingdom is bigger than the church. Hopefully, the church is a subset of the kingdom – but it lives to serve it, celebrate it, embody it, enable it and proclaim it. This message is news that is bigger than the horizon. It is a call to live in the reality that God creates and makes actual. So do you see that to present the gospel as some kind of good-for-you, something-for-the-weekend addition to life is to offer something that does a complete injustice to the nature of the good news? This is not some kind of app that can run on an already existing scheme. It is the operating system itself.

To present the gospel is to call every person, every household, every community, to come and see. To come and see who God is and what God has done. To come and see who this God reveals himself to be and who we can be because of what God has done. To come and see what God desires and does, and the difference this makes to his world. To come and see – no, it's more than that – to come and *meet* the King, to get to know God by name and join in the only lasting work in the world – the building of the kingdom of the good, beautiful and true God.

This is God's will for the world. And the Spirit is constantly working to enable it.

Loving God,
You set us in your sights in the eyes of your Son.
Your goodness to us in and through Jesus is unsurpassable
and beyond our reckoning.
There is no end of telling of your loving-kindness and
redemption for the world in the death and resurrection of
our Saviour, Jesus.
By your Holy Spirit place your hands on our eyes so we
might see Jesus more clearly.
Send the fire of your love to our hearts that we might receive
and give the divine love that is ours in him.
Speak your word to our ears that we might hear this Word
and tell of it to others.
As you address our lives through this Word we are
compelled to live lives worthy of this love.
We are grateful for the promise of the coming of your
kingdom, and
we desire to be part of the revolution of your ways to the
kingdoms of this world.
We long for that day when your kingdom comes on earth as
it is in heaven; until then, we thread through our lives your
golden thread of hope.
And hear us as we join in that cry of yearning for you that
has arisen throughout the ages; Come, Lord Jesus. Amen.

Notes

1 Pope Francis, 2013, *Evangelii Gaudium*, Vatican: Libreria Editrice Vaticana, p. 129.

2 Andy Root talks brilliantly about this in *Faith Formation in a Secular Age: Responding to the Church's Obsession with Youthfulness*, Grand Rapids, MI: Baker Academic, 2017.

3 Many have written on the impact of consumerism and culture on our desires and the impact that has had on the gospel. I particularly enjoy James K. A. Smith, 2016, *You Are What You Love*, Grand Rapids, MI: Brazos Press.

4 'In Christ' is found 50 times in the letters of St Paul.

5 See the wonderful Jeff McSwain, 2018, *Simul Sanctification: Barth's Hidden Vision for Human Transformation*, Eugene, OR: Pickwick Publications.

6 Fleming Rutledge, 2015, *The Crucifixion: Understanding the Death of Jesus Christ*, Grand Rapids, MI: Eerdmans, p. 127.

7 Dietrich Bonhoeffer, 2013, *The Bonhoeffer Reader*, C. Green and M. DeJonge (eds), Minneapolis, MN: Fortress Press, p. 268.

2

How is the Gospel Shared?

'Preach the Gospel at all times, and if necessary use words.'
St Francis of Assisi

St Francis has long been regarded as a hero of the faith. He has shaped the very practice of devotion. And if you have his card in your hand while playing Top Trumps: The Saints, then you are unbeatable. We do well to walk in his steps.

But on so many levels this is wrong. First, there is no evidence that St Francis said this. Second, and with every respect to him, if he had said these words he would have been wrong.

However, this quote does reveal something important – the unspoken assumption that any God worth believing in should not need to depend on words to be known. We seem to think it should be instinctual, or that somehow it will just come to people.

As Chapter 1 established, Jesus Christ *is* the good news. God's desire for people to respond to his love is impossible to overstate. This desire is seen in God's utter commitment to us in the life, death, resurrection and ongoing ministry of Christ, and in the continual work by the Spirit to empower us to witness effectively. The good news is an invitation. An invitation that is for all. But it can only be responded to if it is issued; and it is issued primarily through specific words of invitation, to specific people, living in a specific place at a specific time.

What God has done needs to be witnessed to: 'Witness names the truth that the only way we can know the character of the world, the only way we know ourselves, the only way we know God is by one person telling another.'[1]

The God we worship is not a general truth known by generalities. All we can say is from what has taken place and all that has been specifically revealed. There is an essentialness to the activities of communicating. After all, the word 'gospel' is really an active verb – heralding, announcing, proclaiming good news. The word 'evangelism' has as its core 'angel'. And angel means 'announcer', 'messenger'.

But what might it mean to announce? How is this news announced or proclaimed?

Of course, as we consider this, all of us have travelled different routes with various companions, some welcome, some not really chosen, some inspiring and others less than positive. Some of these companions might have compellingly urged us that it's actually actions that show good news, so no words are necessary; others have urged us to accept the sole primacy of words in transmitting the good news. So let's be clear from the start of this matter: to put words in one corner, and actions in another, is a spurious division that is nothing short of scandalous and damaging. This is not because of what works or the results we require; it is to do with the very essence of the good news itself.

Marshall McLuhan was a social scientist of the twentieth century most famous for the insight 'the medium is the message', meaning that the content of the message we are seeking to communicate and the way we communicate it are inextricably linked. We know this: many times people try to communicate things and we don't believe them, simply because of the means they use to communicate. If I have Covid-19 but have a face-to-face conversation with you about chickenpox, what you will catch from me is Covid-19, not chickenpox.

So as we consider communicating the gospel, we do well to recognize, as Professor William Abraham says in his seminal book *The Logic of Evangelism*, that 'Our conceptions of evangelism have a profound effect on our evangelistic practices.'[2] In other words, the means we use to communicate the gospel can actually negate the very message we are trying to

communicate. Abraham continues: 'Some forms of evangelism
are so bad that they may dechristianize those subjected to them,
or they may inoculate people from the gospel indefinitely.'[3] In
my experience this is what can happen in a church community
far too easily – we become immunized from the real thing and
so begin to feed on substitutes.

What can we say about what we say?

Let's begin with God. Only God exists by necessity. We are
contingent, expendable, unnecessary and – don't get me wrong,
it *is* great to be alive – we are not essential. Nothing *is*, except
God. Everything that exists apart from God exists because of
God – God is cause, source, will and agent.

This God is only truly known as he makes himself known.
But there is no outward compulsion on God to reveal Godself;
rather, only the essential nature of his being. God chooses to
be this God for his world and reveal the truth of who he is and
how he loves, in who he chooses to be for creation.

In Christ, God's secret is declared. The mystery is told. It
is mystery not because it is still hidden and unknown. But it
is mystery to us, it is impenetrable for us, because unless it is
revealed we have no chance of knowing it. Jesus reveals the
mystery – which is profoundly mysterious – of why God would
choose to love us this much. Why would God go to these
lengths for us? Why would God show such loving-kindness,
mercy, patience, faithfulness and joy in interacting with me?
Why would God choose freely to be this God for me at such
personal cost? And so on. But however baffling it is, and for all
the reasons we might muster to suggest to God that this is not
an altogether wise move on God's behalf, this is the truth – God
would not be without us: 'The truth of our existence is simply
this – that Jesus Christ has died and risen again for us. It is this
and this alone which is to be proclaimed to us as our truth.'[4]

And this is revealed to the whole world through the very
words and actions of the true God who takes flesh to speak our
language in physical form so we can hear and see what truth
looks like. The starting point is God's revelation of himself as

scripture witnesses it. This is not just information or even facts. This is about the creative action of God.

God brings into being this world, distinct from God, yet utterly reliant upon him. It is brought into being through the creative and performative power of God's word. God's word makes things happen. Makes everything happen. We cite Genesis and Isaiah, Exodus, Psalms and Jeremiah as evidence of the initiative of God in speaking into being all things – they are only there because they have been spoken into existence.

God creates, sustains, reveals, redeems, rescues, guides, instructs, inspires, rebukes, promises, renews, summons and encounters this world through his Word. This Word is effectual – it makes things happen – and this is God's prime agency in and with this world. Isaiah testifies that God's uniqueness and otherness are beyond question and God's ways and means are beyond us, yet God himself acts in such a way as to make possible what only God can make possible by the power of self-communication:

> For as the rain and the snow come down from heaven,
>   and do not return there until they have watered the earth,
> making it bring forth and sprout,
>   giving seed to the sower and bread to the eater,
> so shall my word be that goes out from my mouth;
>   it shall not return to me empty,
> but it shall accomplish that which I purpose,
> and succeed in the thing for which I sent it.
> (Isaiah 55.10–11)

The Gospel of John mashes up this great Old Testament theme of God's all-creative, all-sustaining, all-powerful word with first-century Greek philosophy and co-opts the title 'Word' to the person of Jesus of Nazareth: 'In the beginning was the Word, and the Word was with God, and the Word was God ... the Word became flesh and lived among us' (John 1.1 and 14). Christianity is first and foremost a communication event. Or, as

Søren Kierkegaard said, 'Christianity is not a doctrine, but an existence-communication.'[5]

Evangelism is the proclamation of this Word – of course, *through* words, but words that only make sense when they take flesh. The announcement and announcer are inextricably connected. The medium is the message. We can therefore have courage and confidence in speaking of this news. As St Paul testified, 'I am not ashamed of the gospel; it is the power of God for salvation to everyone who has faith, to the Jew first and also to the Greek' (Romans 1.16).

This message must be told because it is God's news. And because it is God's news it is good. Those who proclaim this news have beautiful feet (Romans 10.15), because the news they announce changes everything.

It was a cold October Saturday morning, and I was walking round the edge of a field with three teenagers. The high points of our year at St Laurence, Reading were our regular weekends away with young people. They were times when we invited those we had begun to get to know through schools work and other relationship building to come and hear more for themselves about the faith that we believed was good news. Over the weekend we would introduce the young people to Jesus and invite them to consider their response to his call. For many, it was the first time they had heard the good news. As we walked in rural Oxfordshire, I asked Alicia, who had been brought by her elder brother, what she thought of what she had heard about Jesus so far. She stopped and fixed me with her eyes, 'I'm 15 years old. Why has no one ever told me this before?'

This Word did not come to us to reveal and tell what we already knew, give us what we already had or lead us in a direction we could have found for ourselves: 'This message will always have something original to say to the people that the world will certainly not have heard otherwise in lectures, or school lessons, in films or theatres, in conversation or in talking to themselves.'[6]

The good news must be presented, because in Christ something new has been made possible because of what actually has taken place. And it matters that people don't know about this: 'Jesus Christ is the one Word of God which we must hear.'[7] All must hear this because it is for all. In Christ, God has chosen to act for all people: 'And I, when I am lifted up from the earth, will draw all people to myself' (John 12.32). The cross is the most inclusive event of all time.

The delight in discovering the newness that God has made possible is not just intended to be for some, and is not only for those who can make the journey. The entry point is not through a wardrobe at the top of the house as in the Chronicles of Narnia, or on a train you can only get to from Platform 9¾ as in the Harry Potter books. There is no code-cracking necessary; no escape-room conundrum that must be solved first; no religious ritual that needs to be endured; no moral or physical test that needs to be passed with at least a grade C.

But in order for people to respond, the invitation needs to be extended. What has been revealed and achieved must be passed on. The church must give what it has received. For 'where this is not announced, it will not be known'.[8]

'Everyone who calls on the name of the Lord shall be saved.'

But how are they to call on one in whom they have not believed? And how are they to believe in one of whom they have never heard? And how are they to hear without someone to proclaim him? And how are they to proclaim him unless they are sent? As it is written, 'How beautiful are the feet of those who bring good news!' (Romans 10.13–15)

No wonder we find St Paul using the most compelling language: 'an obligation is laid on me, and woe betide me if I do not proclaim the gospel!' (1 Corinthians 9.16). God has acted; we must tell of it. The question is, *how* to speak of it?

Many seem to assume that this task is beyond us, especially in these times. Some insist it is too difficult, society is too hostile, too progressive, too secular. To such a mind, to introduce faith is to fail to read the signs of the times. William Abraham has such assumptions in his sights when he states:

> Evangelism has never depended on a sunny analysis of the culture it is seeking to Christianise; if that were the case, the West would never have been evangelized in the first place. The mature evangelist will be able to take a worst case scenario and set about the work with enthusiasm ... [for] the fundamental sources of inspiration do not rest on the empirical or quasi-empirical accounts of the modern world. Hence there is no good reason why the evangelist should be intimidated by prophets of doom who argue that the prospects for evangelism are bleak in the extreme.[9]

In the 1960s as he arrived in East Africa, after discerning the call to minister to the Masai, the Roman Catholic priest Fr Vincent Donovan realized he was coming with the assumption that it would be impossible to preach the gospel directly to people such as the Masai. To begin with, he had to get past his assumptions that these people were not ready for the gospel.

This assumption continues throughout the church across the world. Even when we know it would be a Good Thing to issue the invitation of the gospel, we can't comprehend where to begin.

At this point we could invite in the marketing gurus, those whose art is communicating messages effectively. Now I'm certainly not saying there's nothing we could learn, or no expertise we wouldn't benefit from ... *but, but* ... while there is an attempt to sell everything else to us – air, water, energy – we have to remember that the gospel is not a thing, a commodity, a product that we are trying to flog. To be presented with the gospel is to be introduced to a person to be encountered; and he makes his own ways.

Our first prayer as we prepare to announce the gospel is 'Come, Holy Spirit', and then to trust the living power of God to reveal the inherent beauty that the good news contains in every fibre of its being.

The gospel has a logic intrinsic to it, an essential coherence. Of course, the gospel addresses contemporary questions, issues, controversies and pathologies – but it's not just God's answer to our clever questions, felt needs or distorted projections. It is not a solution to a problem we have presented God with or a response to concerted crises that God has suddenly decided to take action to address. God is at the centre of the proclamation of the gospel, not us.

The gospel announces who God is and what God has done for us in Jesus Christ. And this announcement itself, its very communication, has generative power. As the work of the Word and the Spirit combine, interest is created, desire is stirred, capacity is opened up and will is stimulated to receive it. That is, the *means* by which the gospel is proclaimed is inseparable from *who* this God is and *how* this God has acted for all and what this means for our lives.

The power of God to bring about new life will often rely on words. This doesn't mean that the gospel is a 'brain thing' – a rational argument that must first be intellectually grasped. No, the words aren't merely conveying information, but communicating the truth of the heart of God. In the economy of God, words make things happen. They call things into being. This work is reliant upon the Holy Spirit: there at the beginning of creation brooding over the waters; there as the Old Testament prophets declared the word of God to the dry bones; there as Mary heard the announcement of Gabriel to her, a word that – when received by her, when she said 'yes' – literally incarnated the life of Christ in her body. The Spirit enables the reception of the Word – which itself brings God's life.

What if this same Word, Jesus Christ, is encountered in real time as the word of the gospel is proclaimed? It isn't that there is some magic formula of words. Rather, in the Spirit's power to flatten mountains, raise valleys, straighten paths and make the uneven ground level, what the declared and received Word can achieve is God's work. The fact that anyone is able to receive the gospel is a sign of grace – it is only through the loving-kindness of God that ears can hear his word; hearts can experience his love; hands can be prised open to receive; wills can choose; and mouths are enabled to confess. If we could get there ourselves, Christianity would be a religion of works. Countless of our brothers and sisters through the ages have insisted that the beauty and miracle of the salvation given in Christ is that it is freely given and freely received.

The gospel has a power that is intrinsic and essential – because this is the mysterious story of the all-powerful God making himself nothing, taking the form of a servant, willingly enduring suffering ('for the joy set before him', for crying out loud), torture and the agony of godforsakenness. The power is not simply in this ultimate love story. It is because it is *the* divine love story. And in a similar way to when we stand before a Van Gogh painting, hear Chopin's Nocturne No. 2 in E flat major, watch as Bruce Springsteen cranks out 'O Mary Don't You Weep', or catch our breath when we look up at the night sky, we sense a resonance with that which is deepest and most essential both in us and apart from us. We are left astonished when we begin to realize quite what lengths God has gone to for us. The good news has the power to re-create because it tells of our creator becoming part of the fractured, mortal creation – a creation rendered powerless in the face of sin and death, for the sake of our re-creation. Never has there been such a miracle. Never has been told a tale of such undeserved loving-kindness, of such an outlandish rescue mission, of such outrageous commitment whatever the personal cost. The most powerful hours the world has seen were as the Son of the all-powerful one seemingly renounced power, to become powerless, abdicating himself to death; where limitless love is extended by the God who chooses to live within the limits of one historic human life, and chooses the most limiting factor of our humanity – death. And in so doing reveals the utter power of sacrificial, selfless, redemptive love. Few of us have truly allowed ourselves to do more than merely taste the renovating power of this grace.

But the kind of power in the gospel is the opposite of domination. It is because this is the Spirit of God revealed in Christ Jesus that we can say with assurance that every person's freedom to say 'yes' or 'no' is maintained. However compelling the gospel is, however astonishingly beautiful, as good as the good news surely is, this grace is not irresistible. Of course we often speak as if it is – 'If only someone could truly encounter the love of God for them in Christ.' However, for the most unfathomable of reasons, this is the impossible possibility. It might be beyond our comprehension, but it *is* possible to say 'no' to God, and for that 'no' to be said not simply because his love hasn't been understood, grasped or even encountered, but because the person loved is truly free to respond – or not respond. The Holy Spirit does not override the integrity of the person in their freedom before God. This is the only way we can make sense of the choices of Judas Iscariot.[10] Or, to put it another way, as Florence Welch admits in the song 'Girls against God', that when someone looks at her 'with real love', she actually doesn't really like it.[11]

The Spirit works in the recipient and in the proclaimer. The Spirit is the 'speech giving Spirit'.[12] Pentecost is a miracle of communication – of hearing and speaking. The first followers of Christ were filled in order to declare the praises of God, and are enabled to do that in particular languages:

This is not generic speech, formal pronouncements, but the language of intimate spaces where people talk to one another … The miracles are not merely in ears. They are also in mouths and bodies. God, like a lead dancer, is taking hold of her partners, drawing them close … Speak a language, speak a people. God speaks people, fluently. And God, with all the urgency that is with the Holy Spirit, wants the disciples of his only begotten Son to speak people fluently too.[13]

Evangelism is utterly reliant on the enabling work of the Spirit both in the ones proclaiming and in the ones receiving. More than this, the Spirit enables the discerning of how to speak, what to speak and when to speak.

On the one hand, evangelism is not a Christian 'scratching the world's itches', an attempt to offer Christian answers to the world's problems:

> In discussions about the contemporary mission of the Church, it is often said that the Church ought to address itself to the real questions which people are asking. That is to misunderstand the mission of Jesus and the mission of the Church. The world's questions are not the questions which lead to life. What really needs to be said is that where the church is faithful to its Lord, there the power of the kingdom is present and people begin to ask the question to which the gospel is the answer.[14]

It is true, though, that the gospel is too often presented as a commodity that seems so alien to many people's lives that it is like trying to interest people who don't drive in a weekend of motor racing. Interest can maybe be stoked in its goings-on, but some people feel it is of no consequence because what is presented as 'the gospel' is not related to anything that makes any difference to their lives. Yet what the gospel does, of course, is address the deepest questions that arise as we live life:

- What are we for?
- What does life mean?
- How do we best relate to others?
- How do we cope with hurt and pain?
- What should we hold out for?
- How do we live with ourselves and others?
- Who should we seek to become?

The Holy Spirit works to provide connection and entry points, opportunities and breaks for the good news to be brought into the real life of the hearer. Many of the big-ticket proclamations of the apostles are made in response to questions that their living, behaving and praising have provoked and caused by those outside of the church. It is with these convictions and priorities that we encounter and interact with the culture we are living in. And reliant on gifts of discernment, interpretation, listening and proclaiming, we learn how to speak of the Word that is given to take flesh.

In order to know what to proclaim there is a necessary double listening – to the word spoken by God and by those to whom we are sent to proclaim. It is only the Holy Spirit that can enable both ways of this open receptivity and imagination. In fact, the power of the Christian story is in part its ability to embrace, rather than exclude, other stories. In this light much in the Western practice of evangelism looks insufficient – it is easy to trace a tendency of commodification of the good news, to proclaim the good news as the delivery of some kind of slick formula or package, which is most fittingly spoken in some pure religious dialect that has become its own tongue.

There is so much to be done in this listening, discerning, engaging and learning to speak the gospel. We notice how many people in the West actually believe tattered elements of Christian faith, and the residual evidence of popular knowledge and experiences of faith. Of course, this brings both a willing openness and a closed presumption. It certainly calls the church to discern deeply and imaginatively how best to speak of the good news of Christ to a culture that thinks it has no need to listen. We might wistfully imagine, with Dietrich Bonhoeffer, a time when religious words and concepts fall entirely from use, so that we might reintroduce them to the next generation without the inherited baggage and with their true meaning. In reality there is an urgent and pressing necessity to receive the empowering of the Spirit, so that we might speak the wonders of God in tongues and languages of those we live among, so they can hear and comprehend for themselves. The work of the Spirit in translation is needed more than ever.

To do justice to this living Word it should never be stale, but always fresh. Not just a recapitulation of a past formula. The proclamation of the good news is a retelling of the old, old story, but it must be done in ways that do justice to the God who came among the people of the first century and spoke to them in their own language, in their everyday locations, and co-opted the sights and sounds surrounding them to proclaim the good news. Jesus is a genius storyteller – weaving compelling and spellbinding dramas that are more often than not directly applied to address the tension or controversy his actions have stirred up. The parable of the Prodigal Son is, says Charles Dickens, the best story ever told; the author and historian Tom Holland claims that the Good Samaritan is the most influential short story in history. We need all our best creatives to be engaged in working out how best to tell the story of salvation today. Jesus' stories are told not to pass time, but to bring about a change. They are stories in which the listeners, if they have ears to hear, can locate themselves and be challenged as to their positions and actions. And every parable is open-ended, so as to demand a response.

And in case it needs saying, we are not neutral with regard to the response. The invitation is offered so as to be received. But while the gospel's own coherence and logic is compelling, we do not simply try to secure the largest possible take-up, the most impressive results, or hit the largest exponential targets. By the empowering of the Spirit we seek to be faithful and to announce the good news of Christ in ways that do justice to his goodness and newness. Ringing in our ears is Bonhoeffer's comparison of cheap grace and costly grace,[15] and his warning that an obsession with administering cheap grace will sink the church. Maybe we should be astonished if the gospel is embraced quickly and without struggle; the proclamation of the gospel is no 'one-night stand'. In 1748, John Wesley and those he worked with decided not to keep preaching in localities where there was no capacity to care, or commit to those who might have responded to the initial invitation of the gospel.

Words in the flesh

Because evangelism is the announcing of the Word made flesh it is – again by nature of the one from whom it comes – necessarily *lived*. The Word of the gospel will more often than not only make sense – be grasped and comprehended by the hearer – when it is seen; when it takes flesh. The gospel is life. For far too long evangelism has been held in the realm of some kind of disembodied proclamation – as if declaring it were enough. But this truth is performative truth, lived truth, tangible truth. Flesh and blood truth. I remember Sean, a 16-year-old young person at St Laurence, telling me it was only when he saw how he was welcomed, shown interest in and cared for, that he began to understand words like grace, mercy and love.

After John the Baptist had been imprisoned, he sent two of his followers to Jesus to ask questions. John's entire ministry has been as a forerunner, as one who prepared the way. He warned all who would listen, and those who wouldn't, that there was coming behind him one who was before him, who would bring the judgement of God to the nation: 'the axe is lying at the root of the trees' (Luke 3.9). There had been some kind of baton handing-over to his cousin Jesus when he came on to the scene to be baptized, rather inexplicably to John's mind at least. And while John had understood his role was now to edge off to the side of the stage ('He must increase, but I must decrease', John 3.30) he had questions as to whether Jesus was actually the one he had proclaimed. Jesus' answer is clear:

'John the Baptist has sent us to you to ask, "Are you the one who is to come, or are we to wait for another?"' Jesus had just then cured many people of diseases, plagues, and evil spirits, and had given sight to many who were blind. And he answered them, 'Go and tell John what you have seen and heard: the blind receive their sight, the lame walk, the lepers are cleansed, the deaf hear, the dead are raised, the poor have *good news brought to them.*' (Luke 7.20–22)

Good news is 'brought to them'.

Showing the good news in actions isn't some kind of feeding the water – a kind of warm-up act that gets people's attention and softens them to be open and receptive so the message is more amenable. I remember a sour taste in my mouth at college when someone explained the importance of Christian relief agencies feeding hungry people was because 'a hungry belly has no ears'. It is just every kind of wrong. No, the hungry aren't fed because otherwise they won't be able to concentrate on listening to the words of the gospel. The good news is that in the kingdom of God there are no hungry people. So to feed them is to bring them good news.

The miracles of Jesus are in this category of good news. They aren't attention-seeking actions or mere illustrations for the words about to be spoken. They are signs of the goodness of the kingdom of God. The kingdom is good for the blind and the lame, the distraught and disgraced, the dying and dead. For the kingdom is sight and health, hope and dignity, healing and life.

The story of the good news is only truly told when it is embodied. Our actions do not merely illustrate, demonstrate or explain – but actually bring the good news: 'it is impossible to give faithful witness to the gospel while being indifferent to the situation of the hungry, the sick, the victims of human inhumanity.'[16]

In particular, the gospel addresses the division and prejudices of society. In our times this requires embarking on particular listening into issues that we absolutely have to change. Howard Thurman, who played a leading role in the social justice movements in North America in the twentieth century and was an inspiration and mentor to Dr Martin Luther King, puts it this way:

I do not ignore the theological and metaphysical interpretation of the Christian doctrine of salvation. But the underprivileged everywhere have long since abandoned any hope that this type of salvation deals with the crucial issues by which their days are turned into despair without consolation. The basic fact is that Christianity as it was born in the mind of this Jewish teacher and thinker appears as a technique of survival for the oppressed. That it became, through the intervening years, a religion of the powerful and the dominant, used sometimes as an instrument of oppression, must not tempt us into believing that it was thus in the mind and life of Jesus. 'In him was life; and the life was the light of men.' Wherever his spirit appears, the oppressed gather fresh courage; for he announced the good news that fear, hypocrisy, and hatred, the three hounds of hell that track the trail of the disinherited, need have no dominion over them.[17]

There are no choices for the church of Jesus Christ apart from the choices of Jesus Christ. There is no priority for us except his. But to our shame the church has historically been on the side of the strong and the powerful and against the weak and oppressed.

The good news is that in Jesus Christ the kingdom of God has arrived, and in the realm where God reigns there is no oppression or prejudice, there is no neglect or favouritism, no one goes hungry, no one is overlooked: 'Christian evangelization cannot take place where there is limited seating or where the table has been fashioned in such a way as to reinforce social privilege and hierarchy.'[18]

Evangelism with a zero-tolerance attitude to racism, sexism, homophobia, classism and ageism is not simply helpful, but an essential and required obligation. Again, this is not in order to get the gospel a hearing – the 'becoming all things for the sake of the gospel' – it *is* the gospel. The gospel is commitment to the ways and means of this kingdom. It is the enactment of the cause of Christ, whatever the cost, whatever the opposition, whatever the implications, whatever must be given up in order to stake everything on this.

The virtues of the kingdom are qualities that are suspected to be weaknesses in the world: mercy, mourning, forgiveness, vulnerability, understanding, compassion, truth, repentance, going the extra mile and turning the other cheek. But the good news is that the only lasting kingdom throughout eternity is God's.

Not only is the gospel commitment enacted by God's people, the impact of the good news is evidenced by the difference in their lives. It was the American Protestant theologian Reinhold Niebuhr who gave the devastating critique of Western Christianity when he asked why the lives of most Christians reminded him of those celebrities who were endorsing products you knew they weren't using themselves. Or, as Nietzsche allegedly said: 'You will have to look more redeemed if I am to believe in your Redeemer.'

We long for consistency, for lives that are authentic and integrated – where there is no gap between what we say and what we do, what we aspire to and what we are committed to, what we insist matters and what we show matters. To be whole people.

The same with our faith. In Stanley Hauerwas's words, 'we cannot speak this truth without it having worked truthfully in us ... to speak Christianly means that the speakers' lives must correspond with what they say. The very grammar of Christian speech presumes that those who use the language have a character commensurate with it.'[19] After all, it was not the superiority of the church's preaching that finally disarmed the Roman imperial powers, but the faithfulness of its martyrs.

Moreover, the gospel lived is the most powerful communication of the message we are conveying. This is why we all know that Bishop Lesslie Newbigin's observation that the church is the hermeneutic of the gospel is one of the greatest challenges and opportunities in evangelism. The proclamation of the word cannot be separated from the community that is formed by the Word by the enabling of the Holy Spirit. This will be fully explored and celebrated in another chapter – but our experience completely backs this up. Grace, hope, forgiveness, fresh starts, value, freedom, mercy, faith, joy – and, of course, love – are words whose meaning we only truly grasp when we experience them lived. And this is costly for all involved. But as Van Morrison sings, 'How can we listen to you, when we know your talk is cheap?'[20] Words and lives that proclaim the gospel necessarily embody the costly love of the God who gave it all.

What we are after, in words and actions, is evangelism worthy of the gospel. It's show and tell.

And the most exhilarating thing of all is that, while we might have a sense of what the gospel tastes like, we are always on the way when it comes to realizing how best to proclaim it. This treasure is both 'new and old' (Matthew 13.52), and few have imaginations animated sufficiently by the Spirit to conceive what this might truly look like. Yet there is nothing to compare with the joy and privilege of participating in the new birth that reception of the gospel causes.

When the LORD restored the fortunes of Zion,
   we were like those who dream.
Then our mouth was filled with laughter,
   and our tongue with shouts of joy;
then it was said among the nations,
   'The LORD has done great things for them.'
The LORD has done great things for us,
and we rejoiced.
(Psalm 126.1–3)

Loving God; speaker, message, consequence,
Living word,
You who have spoken all things into being. In your mercy
   you have spoken into our being Christ Jesus. Your Spirit
   has enabled us to hear and receive your word. This lifts
   our voices as we employ our most eloquent words of
   praise and gratitude to you.
We long for you to open our lips that we may adequately
   and faithfully declare your praises to those who live
   oblivious to your Word of life for their lives.

*We long that you would open the ears, hands, hearts and
minds of those we know who live apart from your
recreating word, that they would be called into being.
May our lives interpret what our words speak of.
May your word take flesh in the life of your people, that
who you are, how you love and what you do would be
encountered, responded to and participated in by those
you send us to.
Hold your plumbline against our unfaithful witness that all
we do and say may be realigned by your grace and loving-
kindness. For the glory of Jesus. Amen.*

Notes

1 Stanley Hauerwas and Charles Pinches, 2012, 'Witness', in *Faith-
ful Reading: New Essays in Theology in Honour of Fergus Kerr OP*,
Simon Oliver, Karen Kilby and Thomas O'Loughlin (eds), New York:
T & T Clark Theology, p. 2.

2 William J. Abraham, 1989, *The Logic of Evangelism*, London:
Hodder & Stoughton, p. 164.

3 Abraham, *The Logic of Evangelism*, p. 166.

4 Karl Barth, 1957, *Church Dogmatics* 2.1, London: T & T Clark,
p. 167.

5 Kierkegaard quoted in Adam Neder, 2019, *Theology as a Way of
Life*, Grand Rapids, MI: Baker Academic, p. 102.

6 Karl Barth, 2009, *God Here and Now*, London: Routledge, p. 52.

7 The Barmen Declaration. The Barmen Declaration (also known as
the Theological Declaration of Barmen 1934) was a document adopted
by Christians in Nazi Germany who opposed the German Christian
movement.

8 Abraham, *The Logic of Evangelism*, p. 171.

9 Abraham, *The Logic of Evangelism*, p. 202.

10 The North American theologian Stanley Hauerwas refers to Judas
as posing the most poignant problem of the New Testament.

11 Florence + the Machine, 2022, 'Girls Against God', *Dance Fever*,
Polydor.

12 Simon Tugwell, 1976, 'The Speech-Giving Spirit', in Simon Tugwell
et al., *New Heaven, New Earth? An Encounter with Pentecostalism*,
London: Darton, Longman & Todd, pp. 119–60.

13 Willie Jennings, 2017, *Acts: A Theological Commentary on the Bible*, Louisville, KY: Westminster John Knox Press, pp. 29–30.

14 Lesslie Newbigin, 2014, *The Gospel in a Pluralistic Society*, London: SPCK, p. 119.

15 Dietrich Bonhoeffer, 2015, *The Cost of Discipleship*, London: SCM Press, ch. 1.

16 Newbigin, *The Gospel in a Pluralistic Society*, p. 136.

17 Howard Thurman, 1996, *Jesus and the Disinherited*, Boston, MA: Beacon Press, p. 29.

18 Brian Stone, 2007, *Evangelism after Christendom*, Grand Rapids, MI: Brazos Press, p. 79.

19 Hauerwas and Pinches, 'Witness', p. 7.

20 Van Morrison, 1998, 'Wonderful Remark', *The Philosopher's Stone*, Polydor.

3

Who Bears The Gospel?

One of our greatest struggles is with our being human.

There are times when it feels natural to us and times when it doesn't seem to fit. Moments when we are exhilarated by the glory of it and moments when all we feared might be true about our humanity is realized. Periods when it all feels too much and occasions when we never want it to end. And we encounter each day as ourselves – with all the precarious and swirling contradictions, desires, hopes, disappointments, confusions, internal, external, thoughts, feelings, wonderings and dreads of being us.

We know that if anything can simply be said about our humanity it is that it is not simple.

A significant part of this is the nature of the relationship between our humanity and the divine – of course, we don't put it like that or even recognize it as that, but that is what it is. Isn't our refusal to accept our limits, our insatiable hope to be eternally remembered and our inclination to imagine ourselves worthy of unfettered praise, evidence of this? This God/human relationship is not uncontested. Scripture's account of our genesis tells how the temptation to be elevated to the status of God ('you will be like God', Genesis 3.5) was too much for us to resist, because it is everything that we think we want. Our greatest and most fatal human fault is this aspiration to be 'like God'. Each of us grasps for it personally, which corporately turns us against one another.

Not only do we want to be like God, but all too often we want to be loved like gods: recognized, adored, revered, esteemed and honoured not as mere mortals, but as those who live for ever.

We would do well to recognize how humanity's collective presumption for divinity has wrecked us or, at least, threatens to wreck us. But astoundingly we need not – must not – be defined by what humanity has done in seeking to be God, but by what God has done in seeking us in the humanity of Jesus Christ.

Any exploration of our humanity should start not with ourselves, but with the one who not only created us, but has rec-reated us in the humanity of Christ. And while we are making too-big statements, let us also throw in that the question 'Who bears the good news?' gets us to the heart of God's agency and human agency, and so to the heart of the human relationship with the divine.

Evangelism does not start with us. Nor are we the main agents in this work. To truly grasp this causes us to recognize with chilling horror how much our mindsets are formed apart from the gospel. Many a time a world view constructed apart from the centrality of God pervades the thinking and acting inside the church (why we think we are immune from such things is baffling). We regularly, even habitually, approach things by assuming that it is all about us. That we make it happen. That without us all is lost.

The history of the Christian church exemplifies both how blatantly untrue this is and the damage that is done when we default to assuming that it is true.

In the last 100 years in theological circles there has been much talk around the Latin phrase *missio Dei* – literally, the 'mission of God'. There is also much written about this theme – its history, its conviction and its implications, as well as some necessary nuances[1] (which are better discussed elsewhere). But we will just flag up here that this insight and developing under-standing of *missio Dei* has been compared to the revolution in thinking that Copernicus discovered in the sixteenth century when he observed and insisted that the earth isn't the centre of the universe – the sun is. Regularly – because we grasp at being God – we act as if we are the centre of the universe. The idea of *missio Dei* takes us out of the centre and gives the main role in mission to God. It is an understanding from which the Christian community should never depart.[2]

Most trace its arrival in the mainstream to a gathering of theologians in the 1930s. It was then that the Swiss theologian Karl Barth insisted on the primacy of God's action, and these actions and words of God reveal the true being of him. God is, if you like, a 'missionary' God: he creates a beautiful world that has life apart from him. Creatures are brought into being not out of compulsion but out of gracious free choice, and God chooses to commit to them in care and attention, mercy and interaction. When the first humans chose their own way over and against God's way, he did not end the world or leave it to bear the consequences of its fatal choice; instead he made the move to call one man, Abram, along with his family, to be those who will do his work of redeeming the world. When that plan stalled, the Father sent the Son, and then it is the Father and Son who send the Spirit. God is the God of, with and for the whole world; this choice is made in freedom and love, and reveals who God is in his very being: 'Did you think that I am even such a one as yourself?' (Psalm 50.21 Church of England Psalter).

The church is a missionary body because God is a missionary God. Some define *missio Dei* as every act of God; others are keen to focus on specific ways and means of God's redemptive work. Again, this could take us into a long discussion, though not necessarily one without significance, about 'mission'. However, our concern here is evangelism – the intentional witness to the good news of Jesus Christ and the coming kingdom of God. All evangelism is mission, but not all mission is evangelism.

But everything begins with God, though it is not just a beginning – as if God just set things in motion and then sidled off to watch. Everything continues with God. This is about who God is, how God loves, how God works, what God does and why God does it. It gets no bigger than this. But there are some essential elements to *missio Dei* that inform and instruct our witness.

First, that in God's action, in God's ways with the world, God is revealed as Father, Son and Holy Spirit. This is declared in what is revealed in scripture, which tells of creation and goodness, of patience and refusal to abandon a world that has turned away. It tells of the election, which forms a particular people to be God's people and be his blessing to the world, the story of Israel as God's people. Decisively and definingly, it witnesses to Jesus the Christ ('the first great evangelizer', Pope Paul VI), who was born, lived, taught, suffered, died, was raised to life and ascended – Jesus is the one in whom 'all the fullness of God was pleased to dwell' (Colossians 1.19), and in and through Jesus the life of the world and everyone in it is changed. The impact and implications of this for God's world is then attested to as the story is told of the sending of the Holy Spirit, which brings to birth the church and enables the revolution it embodies. The future redemption is certain: the heavens and earth will be remade in perfection. This all happens because of God's initiative, action, intention and choice, which God was – and is – utterly free to make.

The second element is that there is no gap between God's being and his action. God is as God does. His glory consists of his self-giving love. While we often employ the protest 'It was so unlike me ...' (probably disturbingly untrue most of the time), this can never be said of God. Everything God does is utterly like God. To get a bit technical, God's work in the whole world as Father, Son and Holy Spirit is referred to as revealing the economic Trinity – God in interaction with the world. The question is whether this is what God is like in God's very being, or whether it's just how God appears to us. Is God truly as God does in the world? Is God something different in his very self? And it's important because if the two aren't the same, how can we ultimately be sure of anything?

We stake it all on the belief that Jesus is as God is, and Jesus does as God does. The line therefore is: the economic trinity *is* the immanent trinity. God acts in his economy with the world and this truly reveals who he is. And it all hinges on the tenet of faith that Jesus is 'the faithful and true witness' (Revelation 3.14).

This is far, far away from an inconsequential how-many-angels-can-dance-on-the-head-of-a-pin discussion – that is, only of interest to those with too much time on their hands. It's vital because it utterly and absolutely states that what we learn about who God is, from his work primarily in Jesus Christ, tells us the whole truth about God. There is no God behind the back of Jesus.

This God makes everything possible. And necessary.

This is the motive for all our evangelism.

For the love of Christ urges us on, because we are convinced that one has died for all; therefore all have died ... God [has] reconciled us to himself through Christ, and has given us the ministry of reconciliation; that is, in Christ God was reconciling the world to himself ... So we are ambassadors for Christ, since God is making his appeal through us; we entreat you on behalf of Christ, be reconciled to God. (2 Corinthians 5.14, 18–20)

Primacy belongs to God in every activity of evangelization. God loves first. Every driver and enabler of our evangelism is God's love in action.

It is God's agency that enables the reception of the good news. Of ourselves we cannot respond, but the Holy Spirit works in the world to create the connections and conditions so that all that has been done in Christ can be realized in the individual and community. In the power of the Spirit the sown word lands in good soil and is able to bear fruit; through the power of the Spirit, eyes that have been blinded by the god of this world (2 Corinthians 4.4) are opened; ears can hear; and lips are able to confess 'Jesus is Lord' (1 Corinthians 12.3). In the fire of the Spirit, hearts of stone become hearts of flesh, slaves find freedom, servants become children and the isolated are grafted into the family of God. The church is made by the agency of God. We are not simply a group who have decided of themselves to come together because of a liking for choral music/not-so-good soft rock music/drafty buildings, who then hope to receive some energy from the Spirit. No, the Spirit isn't just preferable energy, the Spirit causes the church to exist. And the church's *raison d'être* is entirely within the agency of God. Formed together as the body of Christ, we attempt to live in response to the revolutionary love of Christ, which compels us to awaken the world to all that is offered to everyone in Christ. Not only has God done it all, but God continues to do it all.

And so we come to the necessity of prayer. In prayer we give attention to God, not to ourselves. The wonderful and tragic French thinker Simone Weil says, 'Attention is the rarest and purest form of generosity … Absolutely unmixed attention is prayer.'[3] In prayer we engage with the living God desiring to work out God's ways with the world. We seek to have the alertness to discern what God is doing that we might participate in it. God loves to do this, but loves to do this in partnership with his people. And this partnership begins most significantly as we enter into the relationship of dependency and love that is characterized in prayer.

The prayer of evangelism is 'Come, Holy Spirit' – an invocation of the presence of God who is working out loving redemption in the world. It is a commitment to attentiveness that comes as we recognize the agency of God – as the Spirit works to draw all to the Son as he is lifted up. In prayer we exercise our faith, our belief, our conviction that God is the evangelist, and the miraculous work of bringing a person to become a disciple of Jesus is God's. It is not that we have better ideas than God, or God has to be coaxed, cajoled or lobbied to be active. The American pastor Eugene Peterson described the agency of prayer by drawing attention to the three different 'voices' that ancient language employed – active, passive and middle. If one were getting or giving advice, in the active voice one would say, 'I counsel my friend' – in this voice the action is initiated by the person. In the passive voice it would become,

'I receive counsel' – note the action is initiated by another. In the middle voice it becomes, 'I take counsel' – this conveys participation in something I didn't start; the initiative for it started somewhere else, with someone else, but it is something in which I actively play a part. This middle voice well describes prayer. The action is begun by God but we are enabled in and through prayer to participate. It's not some notion that we give God ideas for things he didn't already have, or that we make him do things he needs persuading to do. But neither is it just a passive receiving of a pre-set course of action. Instead, it is involving ourselves actively in the work of God, which brings a different outcome than would have been the case had we not prayed.

In prayer, then, we locate ourselves in the real conditions of our lives and we hold out for something different. This 'something different' is made possible by the work of God, which doesn't begin with us, or at our initiative, but with his loving-kindness initiated in our lives by the Spirit, and into which we join and participate. The doors are always open for us all.

My friend Luke Bretherton has got a wonderful way of describing how he seeks to live in step with the Spirit. He tries to be informed and influenced not by Lenin's question, which was 'What is to be done?', but rather by Marvin Gaye's question, 'What's going on?' And we discern this in prayer.

It was in 2001 that we moved to Reading to take up the fresh mandate on St Laurence to be a multi-generational church that was missional with young people. The question was how to begin. My first idea was to write to all seven secondary schools in the town with offers of help. Pete, who was part of the small team who came to St Laurence to try and realize this vision, thought this was a terrible idea and that we should instead begin by praying that God would open up a 'gold seam' for us. He was adamant; he believed that God had made St Laurence possible and so could be trusted to be at work already – we needed to begin in the places God was working to open up. Of course I felt a bit stupid – clergy always do when someone else has to have the idea to pray – but we never sent the letters and instead we prayed. Within days a youthworker who had been working in one particular school in west Reading got in touch to ask if, as he was moving on, we might consider continuing and building on the start he had made. We jumped at this opportunity. And for 19 years that was the school in which we did our most fruitful work. It was a 'gold seam'. This is the *missio Dei*: opened up in prayer, God at work, us joining in, and discerning that through prayer.

While God's agency for the salvation of the world happens before us, and even in spite of us, it is not apart from us. It is inclusive of us, essentially engaging our participation and partnership. John Flett insists:

> Jesus did not first act for human beings and then chose – as a secondary step he might otherwise not have taken – human beings to proclaim his message. Rather the appointing, calling and commissioning of his apostles is an ingredient in Jesus' identity.[4]

This is quite something. God's agency *is* to employ our agency. We see this theme in the ministry of Jesus as he sends the 12, then the 72, to preach, heal, exorcise and thus proclaim the kingdom (Luke 9 and 10). It is stunning that Jesus would take this risk. These disciples have not gone through adequate formation – there has been no clear confession of who Christ is; their motives are at best questionable; and the evidence points to them not being particularly effective with regard to miraculous works. But this is the way of God – to conscript the agency of all those who are open to participation.

Jesus' command and imperative is, time and time again, that those who have gathered around him are sent into the world to be agents of God's good news. It is not offered as an option or an aspiration for those who are brave or extrovert enough. It is an essential, consequential response to the redemption God has achieved through Jesus' life, death and resurrection.

To be caught up in this missionary activity, this sending, to be given agency, is the essence of our human–divine relationship. We are most fulfilled as human beings when we live this capacity for God, which is not simply as objects of God's love, but partners in the redemption of the world.

We realize our humanity when we engage in the agency into which we are called by God. In a similar way to God's being and action being integral, so is our being and action in Christ. We are not simply recipients of grace with the option of being the bearers of that grace. This is essential to our being, for we are formed for this work of witness. Surely there is some kind of parallel – even though of course this is not a straight-line similarity – between the overshadowing of the Holy Spirit on Mary that brings forth the conception, birth and life of Christ for the world, and the gift of the Spirit that comes upon the first disciples and brings to birth the life of Christ among them, causing them to be called the body of Christ.

Considering the church as the body of Christ we are compelled to assert that who we are and what we are for is entirely related to who Jesus was/is and to what he was/is for. It should not be possible to dislocate or sever the act of proclamation from the life of the community. It is our essential being because it was his essential being. In fact, it continues to be his essential being as Jesus always lives to make intercession for us (Hebrews 7.25). The power of his life is demonstrated in his capacity to form human witnesses. The church community does not exist before the church is commissioned. The call was not acquired later – after a few weeks/months/years of formation, giving time for training, improvement and refining. No, the church exists as this body for this very purpose. If the Christian community is not a missionary community, then it is not a community that is living in fellowship with the triune God.

Jesus said to them again, 'Peace be with you. As the Father has sent me, so I send you.' When he had said this, he breathed on them and said to them, 'Receive the Holy Spirit.' (John 20.21–22)

This is a calling on the whole body of Christ, not just a peculiar occupation for some spiritual elites. However, God gives different and particular gifts to enable the whole body of Christ to proclaim the good news.

Let us consider the vocation of an evangelist. It is a ministry mentioned in scripture – Philip is called an 'evangelist'. Likewise, St Paul goes back again and again to his commissioning to be 'an instrument whom I have chosen to bring my name before Gentiles and kings and before the people of Israel' (Acts 9.15). The model set in the evangelistic ministry of Paul and Philip is that proclaiming the gospel sometimes involves travel – Philip is literally called to the road (Acts 8) – but at other times Paul and Philip remained in one place for a while. Evangelistic ministry involves planting churches, nurturing communities of faith, and all with a profound discernment to the leading and guiding of the Holy Spirit. It is rarely without contention and always demands costly sacrifice. Evangelists are not widely welcomed as heroes or heralded as personalities, but they have clearly been commissioned by God for this task, and equipped by the Spirit. In God's merciful goodness many are called and equipped for this ministry. They are those with particular gifts for proclaiming the good news in particular places at particular times, effectively, incisively and compellingly.

They are not, however, the salesmen or marketeers for the church, pushing the product. Engaging an evangelist isn't like booking a great entertainer for a gathering or an after-dinner speech. The evangelist is not a motivational speaker, a purveyor of positive thinking or a happiness guru – but a person who has a fire in their bones to tell of the love that has met them in Christ:

How secondary, indeed how futile, are all the means of communication unless they're actually born out of the very truth they're meant to convey ... The medium is the message ... which is another way of saying the medium is the artist, or that the artist, like the prophet and the preacher, is the medium, the Oracle, the channel of the spirit and a word which has utterly possessed them.[5]

The evangelist has a particular gifting to bring the message of the gospel into sharp focus for the group of people they are speaking to. They are charged and 'compelled' with the good news of the gospel, 'for we cannot keep from speaking about what we have seen and heard' (Acts 4.20) – open to the promptings of the Spirit's leading, nudging, the opportunities opened up and the places God has gone before, but also highly alert to those they are addressing. Philip is prompted by the Spirit to go to the desert road to Gaza; there he meets the Ethiopian treasury official and, after listening to what was concerning him, 'Philip began to speak, and starting with this scripture, he proclaimed to him the good news about Jesus' (Acts 8.35). In a similar way, Paul in Athens discerned the meeting point of the good news with those he was speaking to. Fr Vincent Donovan says, in a similar way to Paul in Athens, that his vocation to the Masai was to proclaim:

> God has come searching for you. My role as a herald of that gospel, as a messenger of the news of what has already happened in the world, was to be the person whose task it was to point to the one who had stood in their midst when they did not recognise him.[6]

This is an incredible vocation. The church must, must, must increasingly encourage, identify, nurture, equip, release and cherish this ministry. We must also support and protect heralds of Christ – for the reception will not always be favourable. At times many may hear the good news and respond with joy to receive it. Sometimes many may desire to hear more. But at other times many may be offended and outraged by what has been spoken to them.

Before we get too purist and fall into that fatal self-referential trap of hoping that everyone might be a bit more like us, let us in humility recognize that the gospel can be heard even when uttered by the most dubious of evangelists or evangelistic means.

However, the role of evangelist isn't solely proclamation. Ephesians 4.11 states that the evangelist equips the saints for the work of ministry, building up the whole body of Christ. The evangelist is gifted to enable the church to do the work of evangelism. Evangelism is primarily a ministry of the whole body of Christ, and those with specialist gifts have been given those gifts to enable the church to proclaim the good news. Each of these ministries is given by Christ in order that the church fulfil its present task. The prime holder of the ministry of evangelist is the local church.

To engage in this ministry is a decision that each church should surely make. Experience shows that it usually begins when a local body resolves to be bearers of the good news to those God is sending them to. This goes hand in hand with a profound commitment to a fresh awareness of *missio Dei*. It is only possible through the attention of the whole community to what God has done and what God is doing. This is, on the one hand, the proclamation of Jesus Christ, which is the same yesterday, today and for ever, and on the other hand it is calling attention to the one who is constantly at work in fresh ways to establish the redemption God achieved in Christ and the reality of the kingdom whose fullness we yearn for. If we think about it musically, rather than just have the same tune on repeat constantly, there is an innovation and improvisation on the theme.

I am a great fan of the film *La La Land*. My family find this quite unusual as I loathe musicals. The story, set in LA (oh, the subtlety of those creatives!), is of a man and woman who meet while they are both hoping for and aspiring to success. Mia's desire is to be an actor and Sebastian longs to open a jazz club at which he will have residency on the piano. In preparation to inhabit the character of Sebastian, Ryan Gosling learned to play the piano. And he plays it brilliantly in the film. But, in actual fact, he only learned to play the pieces required in the film. He couldn't play anything else – just the set pieces. The irony of course is that it's a film about jazz in which the character can't play real jazz. Sometimes in church our evangelism is like Ryan Gosling's piano playing – we have learned these set tunes by rote, which we always play in the same way. The trouble is that this doesn't always do justice to the newness and freshness of the gospel. For the Spirit is always opening up fresh ways and connections, new and inventive links in people's lives for the gospel to be announced as good news. The church, as evangelist, collectively and corporately is primed to discern these people and courageously make the introductions to Jesus Christ – confident that this missional God is working by the Spirit in each situation to open hearts and hands, minds and souls, to God's transforming love in Christ.

There is one other paradigm shift that is of equal – if not more – importance: that each Christian understands themselves to be a witness.

A witness is different from an evangelist. On too many occasions I have heard hearts sink as some well-meaning but misguided person stands at the front of a gathering of Christians, presents some pyramid-selling kind of diagram of how the whole world will be converted if every Christian 'just' brings ten people to faith (then they bring ten people to faith, etc.), and then concludes that everyone present must take every opportunity to introduce the gospel to any unsuspecting person they come into contact with in the next few days. Then follows a couple of days when a handful of those present summon the chutzpah to crunch the gears of ordinary conversations with unsuspecting acquaintances, often leaving them bewildered with an alarming question about eternal salvation, such as: 'If you were to be run down by a bus on the way home tonight, do you know that you would go to heaven?'(!)

Some are evangelists, but *all of us* are witnesses; and we *must* hold a distinction between the two. There are few, if any, other artists who have enabled so many to connect with what it feels like to be a physical, elemental human being than Vincent van Gogh. His oil paintings are peerless and instantly recognizable: the colours, the light, the muse, the utter connection.

He only decided to be an artist at the age of 27. As a young adult he felt a stirring to follow in his father's footsteps – to work for the church. So in 1879, at the age of 26, he became an evangelist at Petit Wasmes in the working-class, coal-mining district of Borinage in Belgium. He was moved by the poverty and desired to connect and show how much he cared. He gave up his comfortable lodgings at a bakery to give them to a homeless man and moved into a small hut and slept on straw. After a year of this, no one had become a Christian. His choices of solidarity with the people were too much – he was dismissed for undermining the dignity of the ministry. After this failure, he gave painting a try.

And what a witness he was – to truth and light, to humanity and physicality. 'Jesus was an artist whose medium had been humanity', he said. The purpose of art, for van Gogh, was to witness to the light and, with the same priority of Jesus, to connect this light with the poor, illiterate and walking wounded of the society around him. He never really made peace with the church. What a shame this is, all because he wrongly chose a role for which he had not been gifted; the role he *truly* had, as a witness to the light, was quite astonishing. He wrote in a letter on 26 June 1888:

> Christ alone, of all the philosophers, magicians, etc., has affirmed eternal life as the most important certainty, the infinity of time, the futility of death, the necessity and purpose of serenity and devotion. He lived serenely, as an artist greater than all other artists, scorning marble and clay and paint, working in the living flesh ... He maintained in no uncertain terms that he made ... living men, immortals.[7]

The call to be witnesses is not a call to turn every conversation, every interaction and every encounter into a 'gospel opportunity'. It is far more exciting, dynamic and possible than that.

The role of a witness is to give testimony to their experience – what they have seen or heard, events they have been involved in, perspectives they have from what has taken place. Something has happened that they are called to tell people of. First and foremost, the witness is a first-hand witness 'of' Jesus Christ; we have experienced something personally, directly, in the person of Jesus Christ. Then, and only then, we witness 'to' Jesus Christ – testifying to what, or rather who, we have encountered in Christ.

This is entirely reliant on *missio Dei* – the missionary God who makes up the distance to encounter us in Christ Jesus and sends the Holy Spirit to us that we may live our lives in the response to that and every subsequent encounter. To be a witness to Jesus Christ is entirely rooted and enabled in God's action. Jesus' final spoken words to his followers are:

> you will receive power when the Holy Spirit has come upon you; and you will be my witnesses in Jerusalem, in all Judea and Samaria, and to the ends of the earth. (Acts 1.8)

It is the gift of the Holy Spirit that makes witnesses. This suggests that there should be no talk of the work of the Holy Spirit in God's people that does not have a direct impact on our effective witness. There should be no talk of churches having seasons and times of renewal that 'just focus on ourselves' – apart from a commitment to those outside of faith. It is impossible to justify church diaries that betray the idea that what this community needs is simply to focus on itself and get itself refreshed and restored before any thought can be given to how it might witness. This is part of the 'fit your own oxygen mask first' culture and should be understood to be deeply unchristian.

This is a profound understanding and commitment – that the reason God comes to us in loving-kindness is so that we might be witnesses. We know ourselves to be the beloved of God so that we might bear witness to this grace, so that others in turn may become witnesses of it to others.

Moreover, all are counted in on this one. All are witnesses. And it is not a verb describing something we *do*; it is a noun describing who we *are*. To be a witness is a given. It is not an option depending on how we feel, the amount of time we have on our hands or how extrovert our personality type is. It is a given. We are, by virtue of the gift of the Spirit, witnesses. The pivotal question isn't whether we want to be witnesses, feel up to it or have a good track record. It is whether we are faithful or unfaithful in our witness.

In order to be faithful we simply (!) need to receive all that the Holy Spirit comes to give us and be alert to all that the same Spirit is doing around us that gives us opportunities to be witnesses. Everything is given to us in the Spirit – the encounter with Jesus Christ, the equipping to witness to him and the particular opportunities to witness. This missionary God is always opening up points where the gospel can get traction. We do not have to become like someone else in order to be a witness. In fact, that's the last thing we need to do. No one can be a witness like someone else – it is intensely personal and profoundly particular. The Spirit does not come to make us uniform or like anyone else – other than from Jesus Christ, the 'true and faithful witness'.

To be a witness necessitates that I have something to witness to; in other words, that there is a *current* element to what I have encountered – that I am not just living off a reality I experienced years ago. To be a witness necessitates that I live in a way that is congruent with what I have witnessed. However, it also means being free to be honest about doubts and struggles, pain and difficulties. Surely it is the experience of many that God has felt closer when we are suffering than in a life of ease and affluence. The bearing of testimony in the face of great affliction continues to be one of the most powerful witnesses to a world that does not really know how to suffer, how to bear affliction and, most significantly, how to die. If to be a witness is simply to give testimony to what we have experienced, many of us would tell of the profoundest sense of God's presence in the most terrible and apparently 'godforsaken' circumstances. This is the witness of those who are never thrown back on themselves.

But to speak as a witness is usually done in response to questions or remarks that are initiated from others – maybe provoked by the witness of our lives, but certainly stirred by the Spirit. The New Testament encourages us to be responsive as witnesses:

> Always be ready to make your defence to anyone who demands from you an account of the hope that is in you; yet do it with gentleness and reverence. (1 Peter 3.15–16)

> Conduct yourselves wisely towards outsiders, making the most of the time. Let your speech always be gracious, seasoned with salt, so that you may know how you ought to answer everyone. (Colossians 4.5–6)

Note that these encouragements to verbal witnessing are prompted by others. The task of the witness is to be alert and awake to these opportunities. It is the Spirit who enables us – no wonder throughout scripture there are all those invitations, imperatives and warnings to watch and pray, to wait and listen, to be alert and expectant. The fundamental place of prayer cannot be overstated in this, as by prayer numerous opportunities are opened up to witness. It is my experience that the one prayer that is always answered explicitly and directly is the prayer that God would give me opportunities to bear witness to Christ.

The eternal God is the creator, originator, author and initiator of the good news. God is both the content of the good news and the means by which it is conveyed. And yet this God, who reveals truly the very nature of his being and heart, conscripts us – his mortal and fallen creation – to be his partners in the ways and means of redemption. We are because he is. We speak because he has spoken. We witness because he has witnessed. We love because he first loved us. Can there be a more beautiful or realistic vision of our humanity that this?

True and good God,
The One who was and is and is to come,
You who never slumber nor sleep,
We stand in awe of your ways with us and for us.
We acknowledge your primacy and pre-eminence in
*   all things.*
That before us, in spite of us, without us, but for us, you
*   willed to be our God.*
You chose to create and bring life, calling all things into
*   being simply because it was your will, creating us in your*
*   image that we might know you and be agents of your ways*
*   on earth. When we began history's longest game of hide*
*   and seek, you came to search us out.*
You sent your willing Son to be our saviour, and in the
*   depths of our lostness he found us and bore us back on his*
*   shoulders.*
In the beauty and power of your Spirit you are at work
*   before us, often in spite of us but with us and for all*
*   people. Our request is that you would enable us to discern*
*   all you are doing and participate with all you have given us.*
It is our desire to recognize your work in the world and
*   willingly and joyfully play the part you invite us to play.*
Would your enabling Spirit call and cause those who are
*   your heralds to proclaim your good news powerfully in a*
*   way that truly sets forth Christ.*
Would you pour your Spirit out on all your people that all
*   may themselves witness your truth, beauty and goodness*
*   and live in step with your ways. For the praise of your*
*   name. Amen.*

Notes

1 David Bosch, 1991, *Transforming Mission: Paradigm Shifts in Theology of Mission*, Maryknoll, NY: Orbis Books; John V. Taylor, 1972, *The Go-Between God: The Holy Spirit and the Christian Mission*, London: SCM Press; Vincent Donovan, 1991, *Christianity Rediscovered*, 9th edn, Maryknoll, NY: Orbis Books; John Flett, 2010, *The Witness of God: The Trinity, Missio Dei, Karl Barth and the Nature of Christian Community*, Grand Rapids, MI: Eerdmans.

2 Flett, *The Witness of God*, p. 9.

3 Simone Weil, 'Letter to Joë Bousquet', 13 April 1942, quoted in Simone Pétrement, *Simone Weil: A Life*, New York: Pantheon Books, 1976, p. 462; Simone Weil, *Gravity and Grace*, London and New York: Routledge, 1952, repr. 2004, p. 117.

4 Flett, *The Witness of God*, p. 263.

5 Taylor, *The Go-Between God*, p. 71.

6 Donovan, *Christianity Rediscovered*, p. 63.

7 Vincent van Gogh, 'Letter to Émile Bernard', 26 June 1888, in *The Letters of Vincent van Gogh*, ed. Ronald de Leeuw, trans. Arnold Pomerans, London: Penguin, 1997.

4

When Does the Gospel Take Effect?

These days it seems we want to measure everything, everywhere.

We do this to assess,
to compete,
to evaluate,
to decide,
to prove,
to improve,
to focus,
to invest,
to develop,
to begin,
to end,
to prove ourselves,
to justify ourselves and to validate our lives.

Every day we take careful note of measurements – bank accounts, pollen count, sea levels, sugar levels, waistlines, double clicks, voter intentions, viewing figures, fruit and veg eaten, and step counts. For some reason, which I am sure is deeply revealing and somewhat embarrassing, I have become rather obsessed with my daily step count. The other night, my wife found me waving my phone in the air at 11.17 p.m. to make it over the magic 10,000 line for the day!

Of course, counting and measuring can be essential. But what matters isn't just what we count but whether we are counting it in a way that is true to the thing being counted. The number of friends on Facebook is not a measure of our capacity for friendship or the quality of those relationships.

So when we come to try to measure when the gospel 'takes' – when faith becomes real, living and active in a person's life – we should probably put down our watches, clocks and diaries, because such timescales don't just transfer and sync to our chronological calendar. This isn't because there isn't a 'when'; there most definitely is. It's just that in the matter of the miracle of faith we are living in God's time, not ours.

We often hear the remark that God is outside time. I think I know why we claim that – but I'm not so sure what it actually means. There is an 'of course, of course' to God being outside time – this is the eternal one; the great I Am; the one who was and is and is to come, who we are straining to talk about truthfully. However, what we can say truly about this God is rooted entirely in what has been revealed in history, most especially what happened when the uncreated and timeless one became a created being and participated in real time.

In Jesus Christ, time is redeemed as God pulls off the change we most need but of ourselves are incapable of achieving. Time is for ever different – as this work of salvation that is accomplished for the whole world in Christ works backwards and forwards. In an extraordinary way this is recognized in our dating system – the history of the world pivots on the dates of Jesus of Nazareth. But the concern before us is the BC/AD split in every person's life.

In his book *The Escape Artist: The Man Who Broke Out of Auschwitz to Warn the World*,[1] Jonathan Freedland brilliantly tells the story of Rudolf Vrba as the Escape Artist, who managed to break out of Auschwitz in April 1944. Vrba escaped not just to get himself out of the hellish conditions he had experienced during his months in Auschwitz/Birkenau but to alert and warn the world to what was happening – so that leaders of nations would act and remaining Jews would not allow the Nazis to deport them.

In the first few weeks Vrba and his fellow escapee put together a report – documenting their experience, the layout of the camps and the plans for the Final Solution. Indeed, the report did get into the hands of Roosevelt, Churchill and the Pope – but it didn't lead to the intended action. Vrba was devastated by this inaction. But his reflection was that it was obviously not enough for people to have information. Even if it was of the gravest importance. The crucial thing was that it needed to be believed. The problem that Vrba's report ran into was that those who read it didn't truly *believe* it.

What struck me most about Freedland's book was the importance of news being believed.

The news of the love of God for each of us in Christ Jesus and the certain dawning of the kingdom of God is not merely information presented as some kind of report to be filed. Rather, it is communicated in order to be believed. In fact, unless it is believed, unless it is acted on, the reason it has been shared cannot be realized. It does not begin to have the effect it could have.

The intervention that God has staged in Christ – in his birth, his life, his teaching, his miracles, his inauguration of the kingdom of God, his suffering, his death, his resurrection and ascension – is enacted to be responded to. It calls every person to join in – to decide to participate or opt out, to decide to turn towards it or to turn away. It is for us to receive the gift given to us by God through the life of Christ in our own lives, and in so doing to have his time determine our time as his story becomes our story. Of course, society's familiarity with the gospel means that it isn't considered 'news'. But what is announced must be responded to – the theologian David Ford insists that the gospel necessarily provokes a response, like someone running into a room to shout 'FIRE!' or whispering in your ear, 'Will you marry me?' Jesus again and again provoked his listeners with questions, challenging them for a response: 'Who do you say that I am?', 'What are you looking for?', 'Do you believe?', 'Do you love me?' and, particularly with his challenges, 'Follow me'. In the moment, people had a decision to make: to leave what they were doing behind and literally follow Jesus, or to stay with the nets, the money, the family and friends and watch Jesus walk away into the distance. Karl Barth is clear: 'Any theology which would not even consider the necessity to respond to God personally could only be a false theology.'[2] And this response of belief happens in actual, real time.

Of all people, Christians should handle time best: understanding and honouring what is given as an unsolicited and gratuitous gift, living our hours and days in step with the one who makes sense of all time and who works his ways out, not just generally in the world, but specifically in our lives. And it is God who initiates this:

> Now after John was arrested, Jesus came to Galilee, proclaiming the good news of God, and saying, 'The time is fulfilled, and the kingdom of God has come near; repent, and believe in the good news.' (Mark 1.14–15)

Everyday Greek had two words for time: one is *chronos*, meaning sequential time, hour following hour, day following day, year following year; the other is *kairos*, which is a defining moment, a point of crisis, the time of fulfilment and achievement. In Jesus' first words in Mark's Gospel, he restarts the clock by the declaration that the *kairos* has come!

God creates the *kairos*. Jesus, the one about whom we are saying as much as is possible to be said about a human being, is the *kairos*. Jesus is the fulfilment, the culmination, the redeeming and recreation of all time. And so he is the *kairos* for all people in all time. And while he has his own historical time, because he has been raised to life, he is alive now, and therefore able to be the contemporary of every person. He is alive, primarily, to encounter every person in their own time and to compel a *kairos* moment of encounter. Jesus stands before us requiring a reaction.

Our freedom to respond is rooted in the freedom of God

revealed in Christ. In Christ, God says 'yes' to humans and thus humans are enabled to say 'yes' to God. We are set in freedom by the Word, a freedom to appropriate our own conversion, the freedom to orientate ourselves to the alteration of the human situation that has taken place in him. We respond to the one who loved us first. God's power 'unlocks the heart so that there is living speech on the one part and living hearing on the other, the word flying like a well-directed arrow to its target and striking and sticking in the right place'.[3]

This is conversion: the act of faith that takes God at God's word. And while it is another of those religious words that *can* induce a sclerotic reaction, it is a word that, so say the previous Archbishops of Canterbury and York, 'must never become a word of which Christians fight shy of'.[4] One of the most important human freedoms we have been given is the freedom to change our mind, behaviour and direction.

Maybe one of the reasons that we have fought shy of conversion is that it is too often associated with the offer of the gospel as a commodity to supplement life, an addendum, an addition, a life-enhancing app. Andy Root writes about his compelling conversion[5] by drawing attention to the modern tendency to present the gospel as the means to achieve or realize authenticity. And because authenticity is everything, it seems an obvious entry point for the gospel to get a hearing. However, the means by which Western society offers us fulfilment or realization of authenticity is primarily through our choices; and we exercise our choices as consumers. Such choices are what we wear; what we eat; what we drive; what we surround ourselves with; what we listen to; what we watch; the communities or tribes we associate ourselves with; our habits and pastimes that we engage in and express our authenticity. To offer Christianity as a means for authenticity opens up the danger of reducing faith to one choice among many on offer, all of which claim to be routes to authenticity and self-realization. So faith is reduced to the solution to the personal quest for self-realization and authenticity. In such a system only those Christian practices and charisms that are attractive are unashamedly on show: virtues such as duty, discipline, obedience, sacrifice and suffering are all buried somewhere in the 'small print'.

But Christian faith is not some kind of app on the operating system to enable modern life. It *is* the operating system. And only words such as 'conversion' convey the sense of the complete change that is brought about when we add our 'yes' to God's 'yes' to us – and all the world – in Christ. It is the timing of that free 'yes' that we need to consider.

This human 'yes' to the challenge and invitation of God in Christ also requires a 'no'. This is repentance – a change of heart, mind and actions. There can be no true responding to Christ without it. However, the fact that all are called to stop walking in ways that lead away from God, and so are therefore by definition bad news for us, doesn't necessarily make it any easier to change our course of action. The fact that we are called to leave behind those things that have in reality been bad news for us, have broken our relationship with God and fractured our relationships with one another and this world, doesn't mean we can easily drop them, about-turn and head eternally in the other direction. In fact, it may be that we hardly know the extent of the havoc our sins have caused, the gravity of their weight in our lives and the thrall our lives have been held in. And if we have doubt about the gravity of our sinful nature and its action, we simply need to sit in front of a crucifix for a while. But it is the work of the Holy Spirit to lead us to repentance; of course, we can't do such a thing on our own, and the vocation of the church is to keep us to our baptism vows.

In coming to Christ there is nothing that isn't affected and effected. Of course, we don't know the full implications of deciding to follow Jesus when we initially respond. But we sense it is a whole-person thing, not simply a private, sideline hobby or pastime – this is why the symbolism of full immersion baptism is so powerful. What is on offer isn't an idea, but new birth.

Jesus answered [Nicodemus], 'Very truly, I tell you, no one can see the kingdom of God without being born from above.' (John 3.3)

So if anyone is in Christ, there is a new creation: everything old has passed away; see, everything has become new! All this is from God. (2 Corinthians 5.17–18)

Conversion is a new beginning in a human life at a particular time. Throughout scripture the main agent directly bringing about this *kairos* moment is God. But the power of God is not a force that works magically or mechanically, in relation to which the person is just an object; instead, God works compellingly from both sides: in encountering the person and in enabling their responses.

The most famous of the individuals demonstrating this was Saul. When we first meet him, Saul is a Pharisee intent on religious purity. Therefore he was resolved to bring the followers of the Way – as those first Christians were known – to trial and to death. He breathed out 'murderous threats' because of his religious commitment. He was a killer in the name of God. But when travelling to Damascus, Saul's life was upended. Jesus stopped him dead in his tracks, called him by name (twice), asked him why he was persecuting him, and gave him a mission. Saul was not going through a crisis in his Judaism; he was not in a period of uncertainty and trying to maintain a posture of seeking other possibilities. He was not looking, searching or exploring. He could most certainly not be described as open, interested or engaged. He was not a man of peace.

Yet God meets him and everything changes. Fascinatingly, God employs the agency of others: there was an older Christian in Damascus called Ananias whose role was pivotal, and exemplary for us in his awareness of the leading of God and in his willingness to do what is being asked (what if he had refused??), and his courage to trust. As for Saul, he might have seen the light but it left him blind; he heard a voice but saw no one. This conversion is dramatic and seismic, but it is only the beginning, the start of a process of becoming grafted into Christ. The revealing God remains hidden; not everything is seen, given or comprehended. This hiddenness is not because God hides, but because God controls his own self-revealing, and we do not.

Conversion is also the most fitting word that can be used to describe what happened to the shepherds on the hillside around Bethlehem on the night of Jesus' birth. There, unsolicited and uninvited, a multitude of angels – literally messengers of God – came to pronounce the good news of great joy for all people. This proclamation invaded the world. Once again, however dramatic, their participation was engaged – they had to go and see for themselves. They were given signs to verify what they had been told. The outcome of what they participated in is that they became witnesses to all those around them of what God has done.

It is obvious why we love conversion stories, because at the very least they inspire us to believe and pray even for those most unlikely of our friends and family to have a life-changing encounter with Jesus. I do it every day. They reassure us that those who are travelling along the road in anger and lethal rage can be stopped in their tracks, that no one is outside God's reach. This is the God who pursues and chases down, the one attested to by the nineteenth-century English poet and mystic Francis Thompson, who gave witness to God's pursuing love in his own lifetime of poverty, opium addiction and terrible ill health; we see this in his arresting poem 'The Hound of Heaven' – the pursuing, relentless God.

But actually, before it all becomes about the conversions, we notice first that 'the biblical record places no emphasis on the special significance of conversion stories',[6] and second that there is no attempt to replicate them or to reproduce them. After experiencing the change in Saul/Paul, the Christian community in Damascus does not set up tours down the same road, stopping at the very place of his actual conversion, marking it with a blue plaque and hoping beyond hope that other sceptics on the excursion might have exactly the same experience.

We are awakened to conversion by God. A supermarket pumps the smell of fresh bread through the air con system as we walk into the shop to make us to want to buy bread. Similarly, the Spirit is at work in all sorts of ways to stimulate our desire for the good news. It is into God's converting work that we are engaged – this is why baptism is the most potent and public witness for conversion – as we enter into the great exchange of Jesus' death and life. In his birth we were born again, in his baptism we are baptized with the Holy Spirit and fire, in his death we died as old creations, in his resurrection we are raised as a new creation. Any decision for God can be and is only made because of God's historic work in Christ and because of his contemporary work, without and within us through God's Holy Spirit. It is a decision for Christ that can only follow that decision already made for us by God in Christ.

But it is a choice we implore all to make; and God has given us the freedom to make this choice. In his book *East of Eden*, John Steinbeck has a beautiful conversation around the power of choice God gives to humans. It is a discussion of Genesis 4.7; this is God's word to Cain that sin was at the door and 'thou shalt' rule over it. Steinbeck's character Lee gives a different meaning based on the Hebrew word used in Genesis, *timshel*.

'Don't you see?' he cried. '... The King James translation makes a promise in the "Thou shalt", meaning that men will surely triumph over sin. But the Hebrew word, the word *timshel* – Thou Mayest – that gives a choice. It might be the most important word in the world. That says the way is open. That throws it right back on the man. For if "Thou mayest" – it is also true that "Thou mayest not." Don't you see?'[7]

Men and women are able and constrained by the *timshel* of what we are able to choose.

For some, this moment of birth is a dateable and reportable event, as the Spirit provokes a compulsion of grace that causes the turning of a life on an axis. Time is compressed and revelations occur for which the only explanation can be the living God bringing light in darkness. And while testimony attributes to God the role of primary initiator and architect – 'No human, not even an apostle, has ever yet made another human a Christian'[8] – in nearly every case human agency has a vital role to play in assistance. Indeed, we are caught up in the urgency of it. St Paul again:

> As we work together with him, we urge you also not to accept the grace of God in vain. For he says,
>   'At an acceptable time I have listened to you,
>   and on a day of salvation I have helped you.'
> See, now is the acceptable time; see, now is the day of salvation! (2 Corinthians 6.1–2)

We are gripped by the calling to enable encounters with Jesus. We want to remove every obstacle that is in the way so that such meetings can occur (2 Corinthians 6.3). John V. Taylor, in his seminal book *The Go-Between God*, asserts:

> The Bible is consistent from beginning to end in its understanding that God works always through the moments of recognition when mutual awareness is born. It's a history of encounters.[9]

We must be more courageous in this. Recently I took part in a charity hill-walk for which we had professional guides. On finding out what I did, one of the guides asked my opinion on the church's essential work following on from the Covid-19 pandemic. I tried to give a very sensitive answer in which I hoped I sounded reasonable – that the church was an essential part of the government's initiative called Build Back Better, serving society in ways that addressed some of the cracks that had been revealed as the wallpaper came off during the pandemic. But my walking guide wasn't having any of it. 'No, that's not what we need the church to do ...' I asked his thoughts. He said,

'Our souls need saving. We're bankrupt. Self-obsessed and lost. Only the church can bring the individual and societal change we need.' Yes, exactly, yes.

Of course, when it looks as if we Christians arrive on the scene waving an 'I've won!' ticket, sounding and acting all superior, we cause great offence. We have made it all about *us*, when of course it should be all about God. We should show up as those who are invited in to do God's work as recipients, not simply deliverers.

For some, in God's time new birth comes in compressed time – with the shortest of incubation periods – and is dateable; for others, the process of coming to faith takes much more time, a way that becomes evidenced by all sorts of waymarkers (usually much more discernible in the back mirror than the front windscreen). It is a journey that is a gradual development of realization, understanding, conviction and decision. As Pope Francis states, 'Evangelism consists mostly of patience and disregard for the constraints of time'.[10]

Journey is all over the Bible and the tradition. Abram is called to journey and we are told he 'walked with God'; Jacob has to undertake a 500-mile journey during which he encounters the God of his ancestors at Bethel, who tells him he is always with him. The people of Israel are liberated from slavery in Egypt and undertake a treacherous journey to the promised land. There are 15 psalms that were expressly written to sing on pilgrimage to Jerusalem (Psalms 120—134). No wonder Psalm 84 talks it up: 'Blessed are those whose strength is in you, whose hearts are set on pilgrimage' (Psalm 84.5, NIV).

All these physical journeys of course represent spiritual journeys, for in the godly life there is very little that is instant.

Our partiality for the big drama story of conversion is because we like the excitement of it and it seems to be so recognizably all about God. But it is a big error not to recognize and celebrate the long journey to faith as the miraculous work of God. To state again, at the risk of repetition: any openness to God has been made possible only by God – this is the work of the

Holy Spirit to awaken a heart to God. The work of evangelism is to enable this journey of openness. In fact this is, in William Abraham's book, what evangelism is: 'that set of intentional activities that is governed by the goal of initiating people into the Kingdom of God for the first time ... it's more like farming or educating than raising one's arm or blowing a kiss'.[11]

In Jesus' own interactions he grasps every opportunity in the encounter to introduce and address the call and invitation of God, but never in a way that he simply dispenses one set product to everyone. With the rich young ruler he is incisive and demanding; with the Samaritan women he is rather indirect and mysterious; the woman who touches the hem of his garment is praised for her 'faith' when she hasn't said anything; Legion is totally healed as the demons are cast out and he is sent to witness to what God has done for him; but others who come to offer their services are turned away.

Stories abound that are predicated on the necessity of time passing. They certainly don't imply the immediate is the only thing to pay attention to – the sower sows seed that takes time to grow; a house takes time to be built. Fascinatingly, following the evening meeting when the Pharisee Nicodemus is told he must be 'born again', we hear of two further encounters – first when he advocates for Jesus to get a hearing in front of his fellow Pharisees, and second when he helps Joseph of Arimathea with Jesus' burial. We could be here all day making the case for the gestating word of God taking time fully to come to birth. And in it all we note that Jesus is free in all of his encounters to bring to people what they need at that point – be it a challenge, a question, an invitation, a revelation or an offer; every interaction is unique and particular to that person.

We notice throughout Acts that the first proclaimers engaged in different ways depending on who they were with, where they were, and what the circumstances were that they found themselves in. In rarefied Athens, Paul uses more sophisticated language, and quotes their own poets rather than scripture, while in Jerusalem, Stephen tries to show how Jesus is the fulfilment of the law. Often, while some come to faith there and then, others say, 'We will hear you again about this' (Acts 17.32).

On Easter Day, Cleopas and his fellow disciple walk the seven or so miles from Jerusalem to Emmaus – a classic example of heading off in entirely the wrong direction at exactly the wrong time. Jerusalem had woken to rumours of sightings and conversations with the same Jesus who had been buried three days earlier – and these disciples decide that now is the time to head off in the opposite direction. And it's these disciples whom Jesus comes to walk alongside. They don't recognize him for many miles – their eyes are only opened as this visitor becomes host once they gather round the meal table at their destination. This story is one of everyone's favourites because we sense for ourselves, and desire the unseen presence of, Christ walking beside us when we don't quite know it. The details of the story are as compelling as the headline: Jesus asks them what is concerning them, and when they share their puzzlement with him, he speaks back to them their story, emphasizing the central place of suffering in the life of faith – the sticking point for Cleopas and his fellow disciple – and he waits to be invited in.

For many, the 'when' of coming to faith is over a period of time, as it takes time to get our heads and hearts round what's being offered. Like those disciples, we need someone to come alongside us, find out what is concerning us and then explain the action of God in a way we can understand. This telling of the story of God sets our hearts on fire. We must absolutely not downgrade such a journey of faith as second best compared to a story of dramatic overnight transformation. We must do all we can to enable it and encourage it. For this we need particular patience, grace and trust in God. We trust many are being drawn with cords of kindness.

The priest and poet R. S. Thomas starts one of his poems with this extraordinary line: 'Who put that crease in your soul?'[12] And in my experience the Spirit doesn't get creases out with a hot iron. For many people, the journey has been tough and they are unable to walk upright. Sometimes the tripwires and injuries have even been caused by religion. And the reason such people have nearly given up on the journey has been the danger brought to the route by men and women in the name of God. The wonder for such pilgrims is that their previous interaction with a faith that stood for the opposite of Christ hasn't inoculated them against the real thing.

There are many whose roads are so painful and desolate that we do well to recognize the emphasis Jesus holds to the place of suffering on the road to Emmaus. Those he comes to walk beside could not comprehend how suffering could have any part in Jesus' life, which they hoped was going to bring redemption. I remember a close friend in the midst of unbearable pain watching their partner die, asking, 'Is God kind?'

Of course, there is nothing that should be said quickly or easily in response to those whose way is characterized by suffering. However, it is to them that Jesus, the wounded healer, comes most profoundly. As Dietrich Bonhoeffer said, 'Only a suffering God can help.' A friend who volunteers for Samaritans told me there are five options in helping someone who is in a pit of despair. The first is to stretch a tarpaulin over it and cast flowers on top, in an attempt to pretend it's not really there. Or you can shout down from the edge with some instructions for how to get out. Or you can pass a ladder down. Or you can get into the hole with them. But what changes everything is going even deeper than the person who is lost in the hole. In Christ, God goes even deeper in the hole than us, showing not only solidarity and comprehension, but coming alongside, bearing the weight of the despair and even absorbing and carrying it for us.

Because of one who was dead but is now alive, we have not just words, not just symbols, but the presence of the saviour who is always close to the broken-hearted, who comforts those who mourn, who gives rest to the weary and heavy-laden, who has on his lips the cry of abject horror that asks why we have been forsaken by God. And while God's presence doesn't remove the pain, there is in the crucified and risen one the promise that God is capable and willing to do something new through suffering. Suffering is not simply a dead end with no future and endless derivations. The power of God is at work through these most profound times of pain and, somehow, in some way, God is able to bring to fruition his intentions. Many of us give testimony to the most profound sense of the presence of the man of sorrows when we have been in the most excruciating and seemingly hopeless moments of pain: by the side of a child in intensive care, in moments of vertigo-inducing fear and terror, when we had come to an end of all hope to get up off the floor.

It is my experience that for a significant number of people the path of pain is not a dead-end on the way towards God, but there is a profound sense – through and even with tears – that the Spirit brings the real presence of the suffering Christ, not *further on* up the road, but as he reveals himself to be present in the apparent godforsakenness.

The witness of scripture values the roads of Damascus and Emmaus equally.

I've always been a bit embarrassed that my favourite book of C. S. Lewis's Narnia Chronicles is *The Horse and His Boy*. It tells the story of a winsome slave boy, Shasta, who along with Bree, a talking horse, take flight from his owner. After meeting a girl, Aravis, they travel through the land facing many perils, and eventually begin the long ascent up the mountain range that marks the edge of their land with Narnia. By this point Shasta is exhausted and in absolute despair about the whole adventure. But just when it seems things couldn't get worse, he senses an unknown presence beside him. At first he thinks it is a ghost and, overcome by fear and self-pity, cries out that he is the unluckiest person alive. He then feels the warmth of the breath of the being at his side and is assured. The presence speaks:

'Tell me your sorrows.'

Shasta told how he had never known his real father or mother and had been brought up by the fisherman ... he told the story of his escape and how they were chased by lions and forced to swim for their lives; ... about his night alongside tombs and how the beasts howled at him out of the desert, about the heat and the thirst of the desert journey and how they were almost at their goal when another lion chased them ...

'I do not call you unfortunate,' said the large voice.

'Don't you think it was bad luck to meet so many lions?' said Shasta.

'There was only one lion,' said the Voice.

'What on earth do you mean? I've just told you there were at least two on the first night, and–'

'There was only one lion but he was swift of foot.'

'How do you know?'

'I was the lion. I was the lion who forced you to join with Aravis. I was the cat who comforted you among the houses of the dead. I was the lion who drove the jackals from you while you slept. I was the lion who gave the horses new strength with fear of the last mile so you'd reach the king in time and I was the lion you do not remember who pushed the boat in which you lay, a child near death, so that it came to the shore where a man sat, wakeful at midnight, to receive you.'

'Who are you?' asked Shasta.

'Myself,' said the Voice, very deep and low so that the earth shook.

He turned and saw, pacing beside him, taller than the horse, a Lion ... No one ever saw anything more terrible or beautiful.[13]

To give each person the time required to come to faith is to recognize the uniqueness of God's particular work with each particular person. It calls for great commitment, discernment, patience, courage and creativity from the church: in prayer, listening, understanding, learning how to speak, and alertness to the leading of God. We need to ask: 'Where is the Spirit's density in a particular encounter?' 'Where is Christ already present and communicating?' and 'How can we encourage and enable every openness to God's transforming kingdom?'

To discern God's work in leading the journey is an expansive take on what God is doing in the world. We seek to do justice to the *missio Dei*, which recognizes the primacy of God's initiative of love. It appreciates that everything can be co-opted in the agency of God's work in and throughout time to draw people personally to himself, but that God primarily calls his body on earth, the church, and each of its witnesses to take life-changing notice of what God is doing.

For in God's time this world is bound for glory. This is not of our deserving or achieving, our building or our making – but it is the commitment of God secured and guaranteed in Jesus Christ. The screen does not simply go blank. Our tragic repeating history of war, selfishness and destruction will not have the last word. For the last word will be spoken by the first word who is also the Word that took flesh at Bethlehem, and the word is this: 'Behold I make all things new.' Not some things. Not even most things. But all things. We don't have containers big enough to conceive of the full dimension of redemption and salvation for which the world is destined.

This is the journey we are on together as corporate humanity, but also personally. This journey for all people has as its most decisive and critical encounter a personal appointment with the Lord of all time, Jesus Christ. Of course there are moments of decision, and in my experience we can and should be more candid and explicit about offering the challenge and invitation of Christ. Often when I have asked people if they would like to become a Christian, they say something like, 'What, now? Can I just do that?' Yes, do this now, before you have no choice. For there will come a day when before him every knee will bend – whether in ecstatic joy or buckling in mortified realization. All of our time is to prepare us for what is to come.

A Christian is one who has been born again in Christ – life has restarted in that person – and now we live our time with, by, for and before God. As Thomas Merton said of his conversion, 'I became conscious of the fact that the only way to live was to live in a world that was charged with the presence and reality of God.'[14]

The vital thing is that, in whatever time is ours, we live in God's time. As we have said, the decision to live for Christ might come quickly or it may take years; there may be one new dawn that leads us to confess him as our Lord or there might be a series of moments, realizations, understandings and confessions that lead us to growing awareness of his call on our lives and the imperative on us to respond. Our times are in his hands.

However, once we have decided to follow Jesus we must live that decision. This is best done by responding every day to his compelling and sweet grace. Being born again and again and again. Roman Catholic spiritual writers talk about the need for the conversion of the soul every day: every day hearing his call. Every day leaving our nets and following – astounded afresh that we are the objects of his affection and desire.

This is for all periods of our lives. For 'A Christian is always in the process of becoming.'[15] For we are simultaneously sinners and simultaneously redeemed. The whole person is both old, yet already new. We must therefore live a daily conversion – as those who have been awakened yet yearn to shed the remnants of the night. And so Pope Francis charges us: 'We ought to let others be constantly evangelising us.'[16]

Our days then become weighted with great possibilities and potential as we live attempting to realize the presence of this gracious God in front, behind, beneath, above, by our side and within. We give our very own lives to participate in God's ways with the world. Which means the work to which we are called is never complete; as Karl Rahner said, 'In the end there are only unfinished symphonies.' Therefore each day is charged with a significance and perspective that views its mundanities and particulars as God's. For, as Annie Dillard states, 'The way we spend our days, is, of course, the way we spend our lives. What we do with this hour and that one is what we are doing.'[17]

God's people live freely and thankfully, pointedly and gratuitously in order to be midwives of this birth. In participating in God's work is our reason for living, all of our hope in expectation and all of our joy in realization:

And of Zion it shall be said,
    'This one and that one were born in it';
    for the Most High himself will establish it.
The LORD records, as he registers the peoples,
    'This one was born there.'
Singers and dancers alike say,
    'All my springs are in you.' (Psalm 87.5–7)

Almighty One,
The quality and quantity of your love is beyond our
    measuring – behind us, before us, beneath us, above us.
    All of our times are in your hands.
You have marked out our pathways and journeys.
We are thankful beyond telling for the moments of miracle
    that you have caused to intersect with our lives – for the
    moments of utter clarity you have led us to in the valley of
    decision. For the moments of fresh birth and new creation.
    For the ecstasy which, while not lasting, has cut a channel
    for something that is.
We name before you those we long would have such
    moments of encounter that they might hear you whisper
    your proposal of love.
We thank you that by your Spirit you take every step with
    us, walking beside us in your risen presence. We trust
    you for this journey – knowing that the road is marked
    with suffering and pain, mystery and hope, joy and
    anticipation.
Going out, or coming in, may we travel with you – realizing
    the goodness of the good news in fresh ways as we live our
    lives towards you.
Until all things are made new. Amen.

Notes

1 Jonathan Freedland, 2023, *The Escape Artist: The Man Who Broke Out of Auschwitz to Warn the World*, London: John Murray.

2 Karl Barth, 1963, *Evangelical Theology: An Introduction*, Grand Rapids, MI: Eerdmans, p. 165.

3 Karl Barth, 1958, *Church Dogmatics* IV.2, Edinburgh, T & T Clark, p. 306.

4 *Sharing the Gospel of Salvation*, 2019, 2nd edn, foreword by Justin Welby, London: Church House Publishing.

5 Andrew Root, 2016, *Faith Formation in a Secular Age*, Grand Rapids, MI: Baker Academic.

6 Darrell Guder, 2000, *The Continuing Conversion of the Church*, Grand Rapids, MI: Eerdmans, p. 129.

7 John Steinbeck, 1952, *East of Eden*, London: Penguin, p. 305.

8 Barth, *Church Dogmatics* IV.2, p. 306.

9 John V. Taylor, 1972, *The Go-Between God*, London: SCM Press, p. 64.

10 Pope Francis, 2013, *Evangelii Gaudium*, Vatican: Libreria Editrice Vaticana, p. 23.

11 William J. Abraham, 1989, *The Logic of Evangelism*, London: Hodder & Stoughton, p. 95.

12 R. S. Thomas, 1993, 'Chapel Deacon', in *Collected Poems 1945–1990*, London: Phoenix.

13 C. S. Lewis, 1954 (1996), *The Horse and His Boy*, London: HarperCollins, pp. 128–30.

14 Thomas Merton, 2014, *The Seven Storey Mountain*, London: SPCK (Centenary Edition), p. 324.

15 Barth, *Church Dogmatics* IV.2, p. 307.

16 Pope Francis, *Evangelii Gaudium*, p. 121.

17 Annie Dillard, 1989, *The Writing Life*, London: HarperCollins, pp. 128–30.

5

Where Does the Gospel Come to Us?

Is our insatiable longing to live meaningfully in a way that makes sense of ourselves, our lives, and this world we inhabit, possible to realize? Those moments of joy and gladness that fleetingly intersect our lives – is it possible to know the fulfilment we sense in those moments throughout our days? Will we ever find what we're looking for? And if the answer is a 'Yes-but-No-but-Maybe', shouldn't the Christian faith just admit that it doesn't do what it says on the tin – it's not so much Life-in-all-its-fullness as Life-*kinda*-fulfilling?

Of course, such concerns reveal the depths of our self-obsession, a trait that defines us all in these days. But even if these questions aren't appropriately conceived or wholly valid, we do have the means of answering them – but maybe not head on. It might be that these questions are best addressed sideways, or – as the nineteenth-century American poet Emily Dickinson suggested – 'slant'.[1] In considering where the gospel comes to us and where from, our restless hearts are given what we long for from the only direction that can give us that peace which certainly passes our misunderstandings.

Inside

> You have made us, O Lord, for yourself, and our hearts are restless until they find their rest in you.[2]

There is a reason why the most famous and oft-quoted sayings of St Augustine of Hippo are so ubiquitous: they resonate with the depth of our being. We murmur a thousand 'yeses', both of knowing and hoping. We know this restlessness and desire this peace. Even though it comes to us from outside we sense it from within – it feels like it comes from inside.

And it feels like it does because it actually does. And we are glad to receive it, because that's what we need to be given. We sense that otherwise, left to our own devices, we are consigned to have only what we can find, only go where we can discover things for ourselves, only be filled by what we can produce, and know only what we can figure out. And as a species we don't have a great track record of nailing that one. A spoken-word piece by Kae Tempest graphically shows us this:

It's the BoredOfItAll generation
The product of product placement and manipulation[3]

Thrown back on ourselves, all we have is thin soup. Left to our own devices, all we can muster to throw in the pot is what we can create and what we have inherited. But the longings that are unfulfilled still aren't met by 144 characters, Instagram images, wall-to-wall repeats of *Friends* and the burden of being and expressing who we are.

Of course, the fact that we have more options, more choices, more resources, more possibilities at our fingertips this very day than previous generations had in their whole lifetimes seems only to guarantee our shallowness. Our taste buds, informed by 10,000 factory-manufactured flavours and scents, seem to be set simply to desire and devour more. The newer and more novel it is, the more we want it – especially if this object or experience promises to be the mechanism for the realization of that most cherished and prized of holy grails – authenticity. As George Burns said, 'Sincerity is what matters. Once you can fake that, you've got it made.'

We go about living as if the primary meaning of life is self--discovery – seeking to find, express, realize, construct/deconstruct our 'who'. In the quest for ourselves we are willing to turn a blind eye to the contradiction that instrumentalizes putting us and our self-fulfilment at the centre of the world, for the sake of the profit and gain of others. As we clamber on to the empty plinth up our self-assured ladders, we stand proudly proud that we are our very own guides, wilfully blind to the fact that we have got here by being led by the nose down aisles set by multinational companies and their algorithms – companies that have somehow managed to keep it quiet that it's them that gain from our experiment to find ourselves. Oh, and our soul got disconnected a few miles back.

And even when we have arrived, we don't really want to stay. The 1957 American novel *On the Road* by Jack Kerouac tells how Sal, whose journey of self-discovery is the story, is lost everywhere: 'He had no place he could stay in without getting tired of it and because there was nowhere to go but everywhere.'[4]

Longing for somewhere to call home, we are offered numerous places for short-term stays, always a guest of a host who wants our business, loyalty and data. 'You belong here' is the lie we are told by everyone from Disney to Amazon.[5] We are offered visions of the flourishing life that are entirely illusions. They aren't really true for anyone. They cannot deliver – but because they are intent on their own survival and flourishing, for which we pick up the bill, they will do everything possible to prevent us from even asking questions of them – their motives, their ability to deliver, and just how much profit they are making.

It is only the gospel that can deliver on its promise; it is only Jesus Christ who can bring rest to our restless heart. To receive the gospel is to come home, to be found in the place that causes the kind of exhale we momentarily experience before our favourite view when we need be nowhere else doing anything else, that oneness we feel when that piece of music picks us up and surrounds us, the being known and expressed as we sit before that painting whose form and colour captures who we want to be. For the gospel opens up a way of being and living that is inscribed into our very being. Homecoming.

There are, as is no doubt obvious to you by now, myriad upon myriad things that fascinate me but about which I know virtually nothing. Animal behaviour is right up there (closely followed by bitcoin, where the internet is and why the rest of my family endlessly watch *Gilmore Girls*). So how exactly does the collie in the park know to crouch and then run in circles to round everyone and everything up? How do those geese fly 2,000 miles south and not get lost, and don't get me started on salmon returning to the river where they were spawned. Living creation abounds with instances of visceral, instinctual, intuitive behaviours that are part of the fabric of that particular species. There seem to be innate instincts – given rather than acquired – that are essential to the very beings themselves, which are inexplicable and, one might even suggest, miraculous. But as well as being 'natural' they can either be harnessed and/or directed – think sheepdog – or become a thing in corporate or group behaviour – the migrating geese.

I would hold that at the core of our human nature, our deepest drive, longing and impulse is for what only Christ Jesus makes possible. And this is completely logical, reasonable and obvious.

We are set apart from the sheepdogs, geese and salmon because we are made in God's own image. What being in God's image means could be energetically discussed for pages and pages, but essentially, it is a mistake to think of it as merely a possession or a thing, a role or a characteristic. As Christians, the very least we want to say – we are *compelled* to say – about who we know God to be is that he is a Trinity of love. God is love, because Father loves Son loves Spirit. God, literally, is *love* – three 'persons' whose life *is* a loving, self-giving relationship. There is no God but this God. As Christians, all of our colours are nailed to this mast. God's being is in relationship.

Love is essential to our being. To be made in the image of this God is to be made with similar inclination and orientation to give and receive love. In order to be fully human our deepest drive, desire and impulse is to live by giving and receiving love.

It could be that to 'image' God is more of a verb than a noun, something that describes *who* we are, not just what we are – we are made to exist, to find ourselves in loving, self-giving, sacrificial relationships; because that's what the true God is like.

In all our complexity, particularity and similarity we are found and find ourselves in relationship. We can sing along knowingly and wistfully with Marcus Mumford, 'Where you invest your love, you invest your life.'[6] But we need to say more. Our humanness is only realized when we find ourselves and know ourselves to be loved by the one who fashioned us for himself, who invested his love by investing his life for us. To live in sync with this is the deepest resonance of our being. It's our magnetic north.

Moreover, there is an awareness – I was almost going to say a growing awareness as we age, but on second thoughts maybe it's something that fades in us as we 'mature' – (the fabulous story of the four-year-old overhead whispering to his newborn sister, 'Tell me, tell me, what's heaven like, I keep forgetting ...') – of a golden thread that is sewn through our hearts and imaginations, our longings and yearnings for eternity.

> I have seen the burden God has laid on the human race. He has made everything beautiful in its time. He has also set eternity in the human heart; yet no one can fathom what God has done from beginning to end. (Ecclesiastes 3.10–11, NIV)

What if who we essentially are – in our essence, our souls – has been made to run on an operating system that is eternal? What if the true hunger of our hearts is for the infinite, and unless this gold catches the eternal light it will ultimately be disappointed with anything else that is merely finite? We are created with a natural desire for the supernatural, and the supernatural operations of grace enable us to realize the natural ends for which we are created. The desire for the gospel, the need for the gospel, the hope of the gospel, is our orientation – the settings for which we were made.

Not only is this a part of our design – that for which we were created – it is essential for our redemption; that which has taken place to heal us. It is not just something for us to have awakened as our original state; in fact, that isn't really possible. Rather, it meets us in both what we are unable to do for ourselves, but also what we sense, deep down, is our greatest need. Our brokenness is obvious to all; we are fractured and fragmented, hurt and damaged, and while our bodies and psyches have extraordinary resilience and a capacity for healing, left to ourselves, with our own operating systems, we can't fix ourselves. We are in need of saving.

We are not like a self-reigniting candle that just sparks again when blown out, or cut-and-come-again lettuce. Our problems are not smoothed over by the tide coming in and out overnight so the sand returns to its pristine state. Instead, our troubles are systematic and structural, and the saints led the way in recognizing and admitting this about themselves. St Augustine said, 'I was storm tossed, gushing out, running every which way, frothing into thin air in my filthy affairs ... I had left myself and couldn't find me, I turned myself into a famished land I had to live in.'[7]

It might be we are made for God – 'In him we live and move and have our being' (Acts 17.28) – but our desires for the eternal and divine are fatally corrupted and conflicted. The hearts that are restless for God are also, in that most austere of reformers John Calvin's abrupt description, 'idol factories'. Left merely to our own devices, how on earth are we expected to discern and then choose what is right for us when we are so contaminated? How can we be true to ourselves when we are so full of falseness?

At this point it might seem obvious to 'wheel on' the Christian faith as a solution for the quandary we are in. But this would betray us as those who live in a world where religion is about personal taste and what might 'work' for you. So it is helpful to pick up the language of idols here. These restless hearts of ours are inclined to worship; it is an integral part of our natural settings around eternity. But left to ourselves, we tend to worship those things that promise they can deliver what we want as cheaply, quickly and effortlessly as possible. Idols surround us today, but not so much the ones in tie-dye shops with the joss sticks, but in our bank balances, our mirrors, our possessions, our positions and our pleasures. An idol is something that can be good in and of itself, but because it is a created thing it was never intended to take the place of God. It just cannot bear that weight. Nor can it deliver on the expectations that have been placed on it.

If we want to discern the idols of the age, the theologian Tom Wright encourages us to watch what people sacrifice themselves to – for idols always demand sacrifice. And we notice the communal spaces of our everyday life littered with lives sacrificed to wealth and possessions, fame and getting noticed. We observe the toll on lives sacrificed to escapism and experiences, we try to hold together hearts shattered by the trading-in of the familiar for a new model, pleasure exchanged for faithfulness.

Everyone – every single person who has lived, is now living, and those who will live in the future – is made to worship. If we don't worship the true God, we will create our own substitute gods; 'golden calves' fashioned from our desires, to give us what we think we want and even what we think we need. We are surrounded by the detritus of these compulsions and choices, with some of the best minds and imaginations focused on winning our devotion and enabled by billions of pounds. But we become like what we worship, and because these things that have won our devotion aren't actually God, they of course cannot deliver. In fact, we are likely to get the opposite of the advert. Worshippers of money never quite have enough; converts to the body beautiful never feel gorgeous enough; celebrants of the intellect never consider themselves to be clever enough; and devotees of pleasure increasingly find things dull and boring.

Worship of the living God – the one in whose image we are made – is our only hope for restoring this marred and fractured image in us. Our restless tastes and desires enter the discipline of devotion, thereby receiving a rest that takes up all of our days. Particularly formative is worship, which involves practice, habit, intent and discipline; we can't just *think* our lives out of idolatry. In the presence of the true God we learn gratitude and wonder; we confess our failings and receive forgiveness; we hear an enduring word spoken to us from the Eternal One into our present state; we bring our needs and concerns; we hold out our empty hands to receive the bread of life, which can never be stale because it is God's very self. It is then, reset and renewed, that we are sent out blessed to join in God's redemptive work in the world.

Of course, it is easier to write about than do; it is easier to observe than participate in. It is not simply a matter of repeating everything that has always been, nor is it a case of dreaming it all from scratch. But we are compelled to throw ourselves into the deep and ancient river of Christian worship in ways that do justice to the living water that carries us along and the valleys we are journeying through in the twenty-first century. To ask, 'How [can] we sing the LORD's song in a foreign land?' (Psalm 137.4) is one of scripture's most contemporary questions.

It isn't simply our past and present that the gospel plots us meaningfully within, but towards an end, a *telos*, an *eschaton* – the eternity that has been set within our hearts by the Alpha and Omega, the beginning and the end. Of course, this fulfilment is yet to be fulfilled and the end is yet but a beginning. But it is in the future, and for this we long.

Our society, while wanting this desperately – all that talk of 'we'll meet again' at nearly every funeral – finds the tension unbearable, as our Western cultural operating systems are capable only of referring to the continual present in which we live. At times the Christian faith catches this bug and generates the expectation that everything that will be in the future can be experienced in the present. But most of us have stood at too many gravesides to swallow that one.

Our other problem is that our imagination, creativity and vision are shockingly meagre and threadbare in helping us anticipate the end that is the beginning. For many, art and artists are our best hope to lead us there. In every way we must not collapse the future into the present, because to hold on to hope is the most powerful force imaginable for change in the present; hope has been the one thing that oppressive regimes have been utterly petrified of, as they have no means of ultimately suppressing it.

C. S. Lewis was continually pushing the wardrobe doors of our imagination open into what will be. To my mind, this is most powerfully demonstrated in the last of the Narnia chronicles: *The Last Battle*. As the remaking of the world happens at the climax of the book, he writes this:

> It is as hard to explain how this sunlit land was different from the old Narnia, as it would be to tell you how the fruits of that country taste ... The new one was a deeper country: every rock and flower and blade of grass looked as if it meant more. I can't describe it any better than that: if you ever get there, you will know what I mean.
>
> It was the Unicorn who summed up what everybody was feeling. He stamped his right fore-hoof on the ground and neighed and then cried: 'I have come home at last! This is my real country! I belong here. This is the land I have been looking for all my life, though I never knew it till now. The reason why we loved the old Narnia is that it sometimes looked a little like this.'[8]

This longing for what will be is stitched into our present being. Everyone's. Attempts are regularly made to sabotage and hijack it, to curtail it and repress it. It is easily reassigned and redirected, and many attempts are made to co-opt it, impede it and smother it. But because we are made in the image of the one who loves from and into all eternity, it cannot be erased without a trace. Amazingly, this longing seems to flourish in the most terrible of conditions. It is most definitely not just a sunny optimism, a fatalistic 'what will be will be', a glass-half-full disposition.

Václav Havel, the Czech statesman, author, playwright and dissident who died in 2011, was someone who knew a thing or two about hope. He said: 'Hope is definitely not the same thing as optimism. It is not the conviction that something will turn out well, but the certainty that something makes sense, regardless of how it turns out.'⁹

Of course, this longing causes us to live within a great and dreadful tension between what is the case *now* and the eternal fulfilment we have been given to hope for. Moreover, we whose hearts have begun to find their rest in part long for it in full. This hope and expectation bring both deep joy and heightened sorrow. In prayer this is released as we grow with longing for what will be.

The gospel resonates in our deepest place, cascading over us and within us, resonating in the shallow echoes of our depths within a grace that is beyond height and depth, breadth and length. For this we were made; it is who we are.

The gospel gives us a peace that is beyond our comprehension and creation. It is, as Jesus said the night before his death, peace that is in complete contrast with 'worldly' peace. Freely given, truly sure, divinely brokered. The peace is a byproduct of the faith that we have been given, a faith that trusts the God in whose image we have been fashioned. It is a peace that knows that the one in whom we trust is weight-bearing for all that concerns us. It is a peace that sets our souls at ease and causes us to wait in hope for what will one day be.

Outside

But we are always strangers to this gospel. It might be our deepest desire; we might have peace that flows like a river; it might hold together the threads of our mortality in golden infinity – but there is a givenness of this gospel that always comes to us afresh. It is not simply existence that is a gift; it is the complexity of all that has been created which, in its absolute entirety, didn't have to be. It is that this God, the only one who exists by necessity, did not have to do what he has chosen to do, because God is freely as God is. But in the gospel, we are on the receiving end of news that is always new; and always good.

The gospel doesn't tell us what we already knew, or if given long enough with the right brains in the room could have worked out on our own. Too often the impression seems to be given that, when all's said and done, Christianity consists of the confirmation of universal, timeless assumptions and presumptions about the human condition. It is as if it is just one attempt to live and explain ageless generalities that certain types of people can inhabit. A container of a certain shape for an already sloshing-about liquid.

But what we are given in the gospel is beyond us, apart from us and could only come from God. We could never ourselves have 'made up' this God. What a God it is who meets us: 'He lost no time, but ran with shouts of words, actions, death, life, descent, ascent, all the time shouting for us to return to him.'[10]

The Jesuit priest Vincent Donovan picks up on this:

> The God that Jesus tells us of and shows us is so different from the God that we had imagined with our minds that it takes your breath away. If what Jesus says about God and shows us about God is true, then we can only say we would never have known about this God without Jesus, that this knowledge of God was like a secret hidden from the beginning of the world until now.[11]

St Paul claims, '[We have seen] the glory of God in the face of Jesus Christ' (2 Corinthians 4.6). The glory of God in this particular one – this Jesus with this particular human face.

Imagine all the things we see on the face of Jesus of Nazareth – a human face like ours, but an icon of God. It's a face that encounters all the elements that we encounter – wind, rain, moonlight and sun. A face that encounters hatred and fear, evil and manipulation. A face that expresses compassion and deep empathy, tears running down his cheeks at the graveside, and eyes that look with love on those walking away.

Ultimately, this is a face that experiences great hostility and cruelty, a face that is pounded, spat upon and contorted with pain as a mass of thorns is rammed down on it. A face that runs with blood and cries out in distress, misery and agony. A face that is close to losing consciousness as the torture is being inflicted, a face that cries out in forsakenness, because the face of the one before whom it had only ever known adoration, favour and unquestioned approval has turned away. The gospel summons us to come to terms with the fact that the face that reveals God's glory becomes a dead face. As the Danish theologian Søren Kierkegaard said, 'We encounter what we cannot think.'[12]

But it is what then happens to the face of the one who was shamed and humiliated, the one who has been drained of life and was now seemingly as silent as the grave, that breaks the news. His dying was an unspeakable disaster for those who faced life with him, because it felt as if life was impossible to face without him. Yet it is this face – the one whom Mary his mother, Mary his friend and Peter, his so-called follower, feared they would never get to see again – that greeted them alive just three days later. It was the same face – definitely Jesus – but it was the face of one who had gone through death and was full of a kind of life that no one else in history had every experienced. Not a resuscitated face, a recovered face, not even a refreshed face. It was a resurrected face.

And it is on the resurrection that everything good about this news hinges. This is the weight-bearing event for the whole of the Christian faith. This is the defining and seminal occurrence on which the news hangs. In fact, *this is the news*! The one who was dead is alive. God has raised him. God has done something utterly new, impossible to conceive of, something there are no previous categories or containers for: resurrection into new life.

It is the resurrection that authenticates everything that Jesus claimed for himself, which empowers everything that Jesus taught and achieves everything he died for. It is the resurrection that reveals the representative character of Jesus' life, the true significance of his death as a ransom for many, and the extent of the reach of this good news. In Christ Jesus everything has changed. For everyone.

What the good news tells us, and gives us, we cannot hear or receive in any other way. It goes to the heart of who God is; how this God loves; what this God has done for us; what this God has for us; and what this God intends for us. And all those promises to 'us' are corporate. This of course means that there are gifts given in Christ that are not possible to receive in any other way. Alastair Campbell, Tony Blair's spokesman and campaign director from 1994 to 1997, famously said, 'We don't do God.' He said, 'I remain what I call a "pro-faith atheist", not a believer myself, but respectful and in some ways admiring and slightly jealous of those who do. But if you don't do God, how do you deal with guilt?'[13]

How indeed. Our contention, as provocative as it might be, is that what is given us in Christ is not possible to be received any other way.

Because of Jesus, we do not have to work God out for ourselves. We are given news, and it is better news than we could ever have imagined. One of the biggest barriers to Christian faith might be that it is almost too good to be true. In the first place it is *great* news that we have been given; we aren't left to ourselves, we aren't thrown back on our own resources. Who could ever have any confidence in their own schema of things, apart possibly from the atheist Richard Dawkins? Even those we esteem as the wisest insist on stating their foolishness; as Plato said, 'I am the wisest man alive, for I know one thing, and that is that I know nothing.'

What wonderful news, then, that we are not left to find our own way out of this dark cave, but that God has come in Christ and brought us light – and not just light so that we can see our way out. It is light so we might see his outstretched hand to us, grasp it and be carried on his shoulders. We are not left to find our own place to stand, to kindle our own light to see by, to uncover our own path to take. It is given. And because it is given by God it is something of which we can be certain. We stand on the rock-solid ground of all that is given in Christ, which is authenticated and substantiated by the raising of Jesus from the dead.

To be a Christian is, then, to receive the news that is set and defined apart from us, and to seek to live loyally and constantly in line with it. We are disciples – or learners – committed together to trying to do justice to what has been graciously given. A vital part of being a Christian disciple is learning how to be a person of this faith, someone who is not simply accommodating or adjusting life around inspirational straplines or soundbites, but seeking to be faithful to the entire reorientation necessary to respond wholeheartedly to the truth that has been given. The tide flowing against this in our culture is strong and fast-flowing, even within the church. A couple of years ago at a gathering of local clergy, our speaker took as the subject the Nicene Creed – one of the ancient statements of Christian belief formulated by the church in AD 325. After being sniffy about a couple of things in the Nicene Creed, he asked, without any irony, 'If you were writing your creed, what would it be?' I'm sorry – but *what*? I am a Christian, therefore this *is* my creed. To be a Christian is to be someone who joins in the corporate faith – a faith that defines who we are – because of what has been revealed. That's why in baptism, our initiation ceremony (which causes the Archbishop of York to claim that water *is* thicker than blood), each candidate gives their verbal assent to the historic faith: Question: 'Is this your faith?' Answer: 'This is my faith.'

And what beautiful truth it is. It is baffling in some ways that it gets so little traction. The comedian, writer and presenter Frank Skinner gives it this slant:

Mary was visited, out of the blue, by a genuine Angel; she had an intense bio-mystical liaison with the Holy Spirit, gave birth to a man God who would rescue humankind from the eternal void ...

Why are so many people more interested in Beyoncé?[14]

Those who first proclaimed this news were aware that the gospel was a stumbling block for many. It provokes hostile reactions: how *dare* you suggest I need something from outside of me? I am the lord of my life, the captain of this ship; how dare another come to claim authority over me? The disturbance of the gospel is too much for many, maybe particularly the concept of needing to be forgiven and saved; of having to admit that what Christ shows us about our condition, and our powerlessness to do anything about it, is in fact true. As the American theologian Willie Jennings admits, 'the good news is a troubling word'.[15] But to face the light is more than some are able to do. That Plato again: 'We can easily forgive a child who is afraid of the dark; the real tragedy of life is when men are afraid of the light.'

The goodness of this news is that we have been re-formed in Christ. We are re-formed as we truly face who we are, and we can do this because we are loved as the sinners we are. This is so counter-intuitive for us. We live in a society (allegedly) based on merit. I remember being led through an exercise with young people in which we were asked to turn to our neighbours and identify the things about them that brought about God loving them. After a bit of chat, we were asked for examples of the kind of things we had picked out in one another: 'She's got lovely hair', 'He's really funny', 'She does her make-up well' and 'They're really kind'. I should have stood up and stopped the service in its tracks – or at least led an exercise that asked people themselves to identify all the things they might assume would *not* make them acceptable to God. When we look into ourselves and declare the good news, it is precisely the flawed people that we are that God loves, accepts and treasures. The news is, God does not warrant us worthy of love because of praiseworthy attributes, abilities or qualities. God doesn't weigh us on the scales, and if the good outweighs the bad then he will choose us, love us, call us. Instead, 'God proves his love for us in that while we still were sinners Christ died for us' (Romans 5.8) or, as St Augustine says, 'we rest because we are found; we make it home because someone comes to get us'.[16]

This news is given – and the intention is that is it given personally and universally to all so that it might be affecting. Of course, this in itself takes a whole life and is utterly consuming, involving and demanding. There is much we must be re-formed in, much to give up and walk away from. But it is all good news – everything that is required of us to do is so, so good for us to do. For every single person to receive the good news requires constant change. What we are after is the pattern of life before God in Christ characterized by the pattern of learning to confess and seek forgiveness.

This news is for all. Of course, the conviction that a vision of life can be true for every human being everywhere seems to contradict so many of our inherited and current cultural assumptions. But this is not new – this vision of life has always been viewed dubiously. As the first Christians named Jesus Christ as Lord rather than Caesar, they knew it put them on a collision course with the empire. Christianity is an ongoing threat to all systems, all governments, all structures and all cultures. And it is for all of us whether we want it, hope for it, search for it, are conscious of it or ready for it. Indeed, who could ever be ready? Because it is news, it comes to all of us freshly and originally. This is not manna that has been given in bygone days that we try to keep palatable in a Sunblest bag for dispensing to those who might express a hunger for it.

There is a joy in hearing it for the first time, as the gospel itself creates the conditions for our reception. Vincent Donovan faced many in the church who assumed, when he was called to take the gospel to the Masai in East Africa in 1970, that he faced an impossible task – or at the very least his work would be 'pre-evangelism'. This, he recognized, betrays the idea that we think some people just aren't ready to hear the gospel, and therefore must somehow be *made ready* for it. When we come among those who are hearing this good news from outside, for the first time, we ourselves are fellow recipients. Donovan tells movingly of one of the first conversations he had with the Masai about faith:

> I finally spoke out and I marvelled at how small my voice sounded. I said something I had no intention of saying when I had come to the Masai that morning: 'No we have not found the High God. My tribe has not known him. For us, too, he is the unknown God. But we are searching for him. I have come a long, long distance to invite you to search for him with us. Let us search for him together. Maybe, together, we will find him.'[17]

Evangelism brings to people this seemingly too-good-to-be-true news. News that brings the story of a love which awakens us in the core of our being; news for us that we live in ignorance of unless it comes – in whatever way God can get it to us; news that locates us and calls us home.

Frank Skinner is right – why are so many people more interested in Beyoncé?

Father of all, we are your offspring,
Created in your image to know you and make you known.
In Christ our restless hearts have begun to find the peace we
*   long for,*
And by your Spirit we know a yearning desire in the depths
*   of our being that can only be fulfilled in you.*
Heighten and deepen in all your children a sense of who we
*   are, and are called to be, in you.*
Re-image us and re-knit our unravelled being by your Spirit.
Stir in the souls of those who we love, who you know,
*   but who have not taken up the invitation to know you.*

Awaken their desire for you, dissatisfy them until they submit to this invitation.
Truly you are a God who hides yourself.
You are apart from us, other than us, always a stranger, entirely free, surrounded in mystery.
We stand before you more certain not of who we know you to be but who you know yourself to be.
Enable us to speak adequately and witness to your otherness to us and difference from us.
And grant that what is inside be lived outside, and what is outside sets us free inside.
That we may live in such a way that does some justice to the integrity that defines you,
To who you are and how you are with us imminently and transcendently.
For all things are yours. Amen.

Notes

1 From the poem 'Tell all the truth but tell it slant'.

2 St Augustine, *Confessions* 1.1.1.

3 Kae Tempest, 2016, 'Europe Is Lost', *Let Them Eat Chaos*, Fiction.

4 Jack Kerouac, *On the Road*, quoted in James K. A. Smith, 2019, *On the Road with Saint Augustine*, Grand Rapids, MI: Brazos Press, p. 5.

5 James K. A. Smith, 2016, *You Are What you Love*, Grand Rapids, MI: Brazos Press.

6 Mumford and Sons, 2010, 'Awake My Soul', *Sigh No More*, Island.

7 Quoted in Smith, *On the Road with Saint Augustine*, p. 122.

8 C. S. Lewis, 1997, *The Last Battle*, London: HarperCollins, p. 161 (if you haven't read it, put this book down and read it now!).

9 Václav Havel, 1990, *Disturbing the Peace*, London: Faber & Faber, p. 182.

10 Saint Augustine, in Smith, *On the Road with Saint Augustine*, p. 15.

11 Vincent Donovan, 1978, *Christianity Rediscovered: An Epistle from the Masai*, 7th edn, London: SCM Press, p. 73.

12 Quoted in Adam Neder, 2019, *Theology as a Way of Life*, Grand Rapids, MI: Baker Academic, p. 34.

13 Alastair Campbell, 2021, *Living Better: How I Learned to Survive Depression*, London: John Murray, p. 207.

14 Frank Skinner, 2021, *A Comedian's Prayer Book*, London, Hodder & Stoughton, p. 83.

15 Willie Jennings, 2017, *Acts: A Theological Commentary on the Bible*, Louisville, KY: Westminster John Knox Press, p. 54.

16 Quoted by Smith, *On the Road with Saint Augustine*, p. 14.

17 Donovan, *Christianity Rediscovered*, p. 46.

6

Who is the Gospel for?

Is anything more sacred to us than the freedom to choose?

In the UK, we're a proud democracy – how we are governed and who governs us are determined by our political choices. What we want – our consumer choices – defines our economy. How healthy we are has a lot to do with our dietary and fitness choices. What we do for work is largely determined by our educational and aspirational choices. Our leisure time is often regulated with the cultural choices of boxsets, playlists and sports fixtures. We are raised to believe that much of our freedom will be achieved and delivered as we exercise our freedom to choose: who we love, where we live, what we are surrounded by; and, most essentially, who we are. The choice is ours. Our freedom depends on it.

And yet the mere relationship between those two words – 'freedom' and 'choice' – isn't quite so simple. At general elections we tend to complain about the lack of choice: 'they' are all the same. As consumers we like to think there's no one quite like us – but we are secretly alarmed by how often we catch ourselves being utterly predictable. Then the person who is the model of wellness suddenly becomes terribly ill. Or, with a free evening and access to thousands of films, boxsets and documentaries, we feel there's just nothing to watch on TV. And we're increasingly not quite sure that it is actually possible to achieve that most pernicious of slogans – 'Be whoever you want to be'.

We are rightly grateful for choices and, properly I think, outraged when basic choices are denied. But into this world where choice is determinative, to talk of God can be threatening and incendiary.

In a culture that is always ready to be suspicious of threats to our sacred freedom, God can be considered the enemy of human choice for many. It is as if God's freedom is in the red corner and human freedom is in the blue corner – and the two are direct threats to each other; and certainly not able to coexist. God's freedom is seen as a direct threat to our freedom. And so, of course, the view is that humans *can* exercise their freedom by choosing to live a restricted life governed by religion. But just don't talk in any absolutes, as if God is more than a choice for those with an overdeveloped sense of guilt and a need for a belief in an invisible companion to get them up and out in the morning.

In a culture that increasingly attempts to construct its day-to-day working apart from any reference to God, to insist that this good news is necessarily addressed and for every person – and not just those who already display a religious itch – is often incomprehensible for people. And offensive. For too many, the gospel of Jesus Christ seems to stand like a wounded and decaying museum piece. It is the backdrop to those sepia photos in which all the children had the same haircut; when the young adults dressed like their parents; and all the cars were the same make and colour. For many, Christianity was a former staple of a home-grown diet that might have kept people alive during the war, but since then our palates have exploded through the kitchen ceiling. Of course, as long as it doesn't really harm any-one – although the jury is out on that one – and if you like that kind of thing, many feel it's quite touching that some people still find meaning in the old ways (for example, there are two girls in the local reception class called Ethel).

Isn't the answer to 'Who is the gospel for?' in the algorithms?

Of course, if the work of evangelism is marketing and the aim is an exponential increase in the take-up of the product, then it might be fitting to consider who we should set in our sights as those who might be 'most likely' to have an inclination to this kind of thing. Who might have the desire – or at least be open to thinking about it? Where's the low-hanging spiritual fruit?

But here's the thing; who the gospel is for *is* about desire and choice; it *is* about particularity and a personal inclination. But just not ours; rather, it's about God's desire and choice, God's particularity and personal inclination.

What we are dealing with concerning the gospel is the very stuff of life. This is not some fit-it-yourself conservatory to attach to the house of life, which brings an extra bit of sun if you are facing in the right direction. This is about salvation – rescued life, changed existence, renewed being, world without end. And who it is for is not set by who wants it, but the one who gives it.

We begin, then, with God's desire for us – there is no one who isn't on God's guest list. St Paul states uncompromisingly that what God has done in Christ is for everyone: 'God our Saviour, who desires everyone to be saved and to come to the knowledge of the truth' (1 Timothy 2.3–4).

God's desire is for loving, trusting, faithful relationship with everyone. This world and everyone in it matters to God. There is no one excluded from the work of God in Jesus Christ, therefore the invitation is extended to everyone. There is much we could call in support of this: the creation of all people in God's image; the universal human need for God; and the state of the world. But the only reason that stands up is the reason given by God – God's own free choice to save.

There are patterns of God's acting throughout scripture that become obvious themes once they are drawn to our attention. One of the most prevalent is the way God chooses to work through the particular for the universal; how God chooses to bless everyone, but does this through an individual. And this begins at the beginning.

If we read chapter 11 of Genesis we will see that the outlook is, to say the least, not very promising. The impact of the decision of humans to turn away from God and God's ways – to be their own god – impacted them and God. Feeling shame, they hide; they passed responsibility on to others and were cursed with mutual antagonism as they were expelled from Eden. This fall ruptured their families (Cain murders Abel); it nearly caused the end of the non-human creation (Noah and the flood); and soon all the nations on earth were brought down (the tower of Babel). This left the nations of the world in turmoil, unable to communicate, incapable of working together and set on securing their own borders and safety whatever the cost.

The world labours under the curse of all that it has brought on itself through its wilful disobedience and choice against God.

Faced with the heartbreaking tragedy of how it turned out, God chose to act. This time God did not send another flood. He did not find those who were for him and airlift them out of harm's way. Neither does he build a protective wall around them or simply destroy the troublemakers. Instead he calls one man and his family into relationship to transform the curse into a blessing:

> Now the LORD said to Abram, 'Go from your country and your kindred and your father's house to the land that I will show you. I will make of you a great nation, and I will bless you, and make your name great, so that you will be a blessing. I will bless those who bless you, and the one who curses you I will curse; and in you all the families of the earth shall be blessed.'
> So Abram went, as the LORD had told him. (Genesis 12.1–4)

The call comes to particular people at a particular time; Abram and his family were chosen. But the choosing of them wasn't at the exclusion of others, as if God only wanted to bless one family/people. Rather, the choice for them was, in its entirety, that through them God might effect blessing for others. This blessing is universal – it is for all the families of the earth, but God enacted that blessing through this particular family. So we learn God's ways with the world – God works for all but does that through the specific. There aren't so many generalities. Rather, there are particulars. We could spend 40 days and nights tracing this theme throughout the Old Testament – it happened in patriarchs, judges, prophets, priests, kings and the whole nation; these people were called to be God's own Son, to bear and bring his light to all the nations of the earth.

Another 870 pages further in and we witness the taking flesh of the eternal Word of God. This is something entirely in keeping with the character of God's pattern of work in the world, but also entirely new. But now what has been affectionately coined as the scandal of particularity gets its full airing: God chooses to come in Jesus Christ and, in this unique one, God chooses to change everything for everyone.

This is a revelation. What is revealed can only be known and experienced because it is revealed. And the fact that it is revealed is a substantive part of the mystery. God freely, and from all eternity, elects and chooses – compelled only by divine love – to come as the Saviour of the world, as the Word incarnate. In Jesus of Nazareth, God chooses to take the greatest risk ever taken: the one through whom all things were created becoming a created being; the true God eternally before and after all things becoming an actual human in the actual material world – that the actual stuff of this earth might be redeemed.

Jesus is the chosen one, the Christ, the one through whom God chooses to act. God chooses in Jesus to share our flesh, to know our weakness, to comprehend our mortality, to experience suffering, to face every temptation and trial that is common to our humanity. This happens in every detail of Jesus' life. It reveals the extent of God's desire for us. Such is God's divine longing for us that, in Christ, God elects to be born for us, to teach for us, to suffer for us, to die for us, to be raised for us, to ascend for us and to pray for us at the right hand of the Father. Such is God's divine commitment to be with us that he elects in Christ to leave the glory of heaven to experience the contingency of this precarious life, sharing in poverty, rejection, betrayal, lies, pain, abandonment, judgement, condemnation and hell. There is no end of telling of the lengths that God will go to or the personal investment and cost that it entails.

Not only does God choose to be this God for us, he chooses to represent every single person in Christ. This Jesus is the representative of every human being. He does this in the particularities of this one life; and even though it is the very stuff of his humanity that means he is able to be our representative, it is his sharing of our fallen nature that enables him to embody us – rather than his maleness, his singleness, his Jewishness or his being an Aramaic speaker.

God makes the decision, through Jesus of Nazareth, to choose to share our humanity, and in him God chooses to bear it to the end. Not only does God elect to live in solidarity with those he has made, experiencing the essence of human existence, God chooses to bear the consequences of the curse that our wilful disobedience – against God – had brought on to our own heads and hearts. The curse that has and continues to characterize all of creation is not retracted. It is absorbed and reversed by being borne. Here the promise is fulfilled that blessing will prevail over the curse. It does so when the seed of Abraham, the one that Matthew's Gospel begins by singling out as a descendant of the great patriarch, becomes 'a curse for us ... in order that in Christ Jesus the blessing of Abraham might come to the Gentiles' (Galatians 3.13–14). All that was rightly and fairly ours becomes astoundingly and unfairly his. John Calvin talks about a great exchange – as Jesus becomes what we were, so we might become what he is. God chooses in Christ to bear all the consequences of our wrongdoing, to be judged in our place, to be the godforsaken and abandoned, to be the great sinner whose death is caused by the sin of the world.

In Jesus Christ, God chooses to experience our death, our judgement, our punishment, our separation, our hell. In him, God's decision is for all of us no matter the cost: 'The deepest secret of his relationship to all people, and all things, lies in his death.'[1] There is no one's sin that is not borne; there is no one's judgement that is not taken; there is no one's price that isn't paid; there is no one's separation that he does not experience; there is no one's death he doesn't die.

This election – this choice to do this for us – happens apart from us and without us. It is absolutely unconditional on us – it is not reliant on anything we do or bring, apart from our fallen, corrupt and helpless humanity. It is based solely and entirely in God's free decision. This did not have to be so. Without any obligation, God has bound himself to love humanity with the greatest love imaginable. This much God has done. We cannot reverse or change this decision of God. It is accomplished.

This is a choice of grace, so it cannot be lost. It is gift, not achievement; loving-kindness, not merit; it is received, not earned. It is not without conflict, disbelief or doubt – but it cannot be overturned. All this has been done for each of us by God in this Jesus.

This is the scandal of particularity, that in this one particular person, God has chosen to act for the whole world. There is no one who is not included in this. There is no one who is not loved in Christ. There is no one that God doesn't say both 'No!' and 'Yes!' to. The gospel is for everyone because in Jesus Christ, God has acted to change everything for everyone. God has elected to be everyone's God, every person's redeemer, everybody's Saviour. God works through the one for all, for the universal through the particular.

Because this has happened for all of us there must be no one excluded from hearing what has taken place for them.

But while this has taken place for all, it is not forced on all – it can be refused. People can resist divine election. It is not an obedient people he chooses; it is an obdurate people. Unbelief, hardheartedness and disobedience typify the stories of the people of God. And while this rejection itself has been chosen and taken up in Jesus Christ, it is still a real possibility for individuals themselves to choose. There could be no rational reason for saying a 'no' to God's eternal 'yes'. But the mystery of unbelief cannot simply be rationalized away. However baffling it is to us, and however heartbreaking to God, grace is not irresistible. Sin is so illogical and perplexing. Why would any of us choose to bring such devastation upon ourselves? But astonishingly, we know it is possible to refuse; and it is possible to say 'no' to God not only out of ignorance or not quite 'getting it'. It is possible to look God in the eye, be on the receiving end of his love, and say 'no'. It seems – no, *more than that* it *is* – entirely unnecessary and senseless, but there is the option to depart from the God who loves us. God lets people leave.

However, such freedom to say 'no' does not change God's will for all people to come into that which God has made possible through what has actually been done. God does this in the animating work of the Holy Spirit who relates, and brings to effect, all done in the history of Christ into the individual; his story becomes our story. By the Spirit we hear the good news directed not just to everyone, but *particularly* to us; it is personalized to us, calling us by name and enabling us to respond by calling out to God by name. The Spirit works, then, to apply the gospel to each and every one of us – bringing us news that we could never have imagined and is almost too good to be true: in Christ, we have been chosen as the objects of God's saving love. But God never paints by numbers with the Spirit, and every canvas will look different.

The timelessness and universality of the gospel is personalized to each one of us by the Spirit. The Spirit enables each individual, as the person they are before God, to gain traction on this love, and for this love to be known as theirs. It leads St Augustine to state, 'God loves each of us as if there were only one of us' (*Confessions* 3.11.19).

This puts in our sights the individual, the particular person, one with a specific name and distinct face: 'God comes to us, one at a time, specifically, uniquely in the singularity that is our life ... this coming is a call.'[2]

Back in the day in my teenage years at big Christian jamborees it was a fairly regular occurrence to hear someone from a stage guaranteeing that a time was coming when countless numbers would come to faith; the days of 'fishing with a line' were over; it was time for 'the nets'! We waited and waited, but the nets never filled. There might be many reasons for this, some that we know and many more we have yet to discern. Personally, I don't think it is because there aren't times when great numbers could – or even will – come to faith. Such a time is utterly reliant upon the free sovereign work of God. In God's grace, when that time does happen, we will find that the shoal in the net – the multitude – is made up of particular people who are responding personally to the intimate call they heard. Each will be unique in the specifics of what they are responding to and why. It's not that there is a rule to which there are exceptions. There are *only* exceptions.

We see this through scripture – God interacts with everyone differently. Men and women are called by name because they are known and they are encountered in certain ways because of who they are and what their life consists of. There is Moses, the man so consumed by his anger that he destroys the life of an Egyptian, and is called by name by God from a bush that burns with flames of fire that do not consume. There is the Samaritan woman who draws water from the well but chooses to do this when she can avoid everyone because of her past; she is met by Jesus, who assures her that he knows everything about her and only he can give living water. Jesus travels across the sea to meet the man chained up among the graves on the Gerasene beach plagued by legions of demons; he calls him by name and counts his life as being worth more than 2,000 pigs. Think of the names of those Jesus meets through the Gospels: Simeon, Anna, Simon, Matthew, Andrew, James, Jairus, Bartimaeus, Nicodemus, Mary, Martha, Lazarus, Zacchaeus, Mary, Philip, Peter, Joseph, Barabbas, Pilate, Caiaphas, Judas, Simon from Cyrene, Cleopas, Thomas and, that most prominent of figures in the fourth Gospel, John, 'the disciple whom Jesus loved'. Not, I think, some kind of proud boast, but a way the Gospel writer desires each person to cast themselves, that we might paint ourselves in on the action, for each of us is the one whom Jesus particularly loves.

The gospel is for every person. No one is excluded. Evangelism is the continuation of Jesus' practice in his earthly ministry of leaving the 99 sheep on the hillside and going off to find the lost sheep whatever the cost – although our tendency as a church is often to stick with the one individual we have and leave the 99 to wander off. But what God has done in Christ is for every person; it *matters* that the majority of those who have ever lived do not know about it. If what we say is what we believe, that God truly has done this for all, then people must be told; they must be brought in on it. It matters that people know. It is always personal, always specific, always particular. And it is always freeing.

To return to our opening theme, of course we long for freedom – for this we were made. But our true freedom is not determined by our political, economic, physical, environmental or professional states, however preferred they might be. Our freedom is a gift of the God who from all eternity has freely chosen to be our God, our Saviour, our redeemer, our rescuer and our friend. Freedom isn't being able to do anything we want. It's surely being able to love, truly love, without our self-ishness getting in the way; to truly love another not for what we gain, but for what we can give; loving them for their own sake. Such a condition of freedom is only possible when we have been turned from our sin and remade.

This is God's desire for every person, and for all people.

All people

The gospel is universal. While respecting, upholding, enhancing and realizing our particularity, it also sets us free from a self-obsessed society whose only function is as the supporting cast in the drama in which I am in the centre:

> If each human being is to be ultimately understood as an independent spiritual monad, then salvation could only be through an action directed impartially to each and all. But if the truly human is found in the shared reality of mutual and

collective responsibility that the Bible envisages, then salvation must be an action that binds us together and restores for us the true mutual relation to each other and the true shared relation to the world of nature.[3]

God's call is personal, but it is that we might belong – to know ourselves to be part of God's people; that we become those who are defined, characterized and determined as part of God's family. For this we were made and brought into being, and only when we know this has come to pass and it begins to be our reality, have we realized that for which we were brought into existence. This is what Jesus does – gathers a people. Our salvation is bound up with the salvation of others.

This is clear throughout scripture – the international scene of Genesis 11 where the nations are in uproar is addressed by the blessing that will come to the world through the people of God. God overcomes boundary and border. All the nations belong to Yahweh. God's people aren't recalled to the Ark to escape, but sent into the world to be God's agents of blessing and healing to all the 'families of earth'. This promise is repeated throughout the Old Testament. There is the widest horizon possible for God's work and intention. Again and again the cry goes up in the Psalms that Yahweh's ways would be known across the whole earth, in all nations: 'Let the peoples praise you, O God ... let all the ends of the earth revere him' (Psalm 67.5–7).

Everything that Yahweh does for Israel is done so God might be known throughout the nations; the Red Sea is split for Israel to cross 'so that all the peoples of the earth may know that the hand of the LORD is mighty' (Joshua 4.24). By the time we reach Isaiah the vision could not be bigger:

Turn to me and be saved, all the ends of the earth! For I am God, and there is no other ... 'To me every knee shall bow, every tongue shall swear.' (Isaiah 45.22–23)

This universal call to belong is made by, and issued by, those who know they belong to God – which in itself is testimony to the graciousness and loving-kindness of a God who chooses as the objects of his favour the weak, not the strong, the small, not the significant.

And so it continues with the followers of Jesus – the renewed and reformed family of God, not a new community replacing the people of God. It is not surrogates or proxies, but a recalled people of God, grafted in and sent as the Father sent the Son, through whom the blessing of God through the chosen one is extended and brought to all: the foolish, low, weak and despised sent to witness to the wisdom and strength of God in Christ.

God's desire is for all he has made to come into relationship with him, a reality that is only possible by, and because of, Christ. However, what do we do with the fact that the vast majority of people who have ever lived have never heard the name Jesus Christ, let alone have heard the gospel in a way they can comprehend and respond to? If God actually desires all people to be saved, then it is reasonable to look for ways that God might fulfil that. Lesslie Newbigin was bishop in India and writes with profound experience and wisdom on this:

> If redemption by Jesus objectively provides for the salvation of every human being and if God intends this salvation to be genuinely universal, it must be possible for every individual, regardless of history, geography and culture to receive that salvation.[4]

Throughout scripture we meet those who are outside of Israel yet are somehow caught up in the work of God – Melchizedek, Balaam, Job, Ruth, Naaman, Rahab and Cornelius are prominent examples for us. These are ones with whom God speaks; God responds to their prayers; God blesses and meets them in places physical and historical that are beyond the bounds. Yet they are counted in, and more often than not play a pivotal role in what God is doing.

But can people receive the gift without knowing the giver? What is the nature of the good news for those of other faiths? I tentatively offer some rather unsophisticated thoughts.

Fundamentally, there is nothing that can be or should be easily, quickly or simply said about this. Much has been written by experts and practitioners, which holds the complexity and orthodoxy of faith alongside integrity and wisdom.[5] There is a long and dedicated discourse between proponents of other faiths built on trusting and honest relationships. This is going on today and has been for years!

Of course, evangelism is going to look different in each contact, relationship and conversation with those of other faiths. And then there is the particularity and integrity of every person, every group, in each circumstance that must be upheld and respected. Yet to say nothing here is not an option. Out of 13,000 parishes in the Church of England, over 1,000 have populations in which more than 10 per cent are people of other faiths. While this is not a new phenomenon for the church, it might be that it does meet our generation in a new way. What can we say about the way that the gospel might interact with other faiths?

As we consider this, it is vital not to look away from the racism, oppression and exploitation that Western Christianity has not just a history of, but an ongoing affiliation with. The fact that these things are devastating and shameful must not excuse our engagement with what must be done as fruit of true repentance. Of course, Christianity's colonialism, its attempts to forge Christian nations, its slavery, its geography, its stealing and co-opting of land, its treatment of indigenous people, its drive for literacy and translation, mean Christian missionary movements are deeply implicated in the invention of race. We must resist the temptation to defend and exceptionalize.

Take, for example, Willie Jennings's theology of Israel (which is diametrically opposed to supersessionism – the idea that the Christian church has replaced or superseded the Jews and the nation of Israel by assuming the role of being God's covenanted people) as vital for the realization of a prophetic Christian theology today. For Christianity is intimately joined to Israel. Jennings says it is Israel that should be held as the primary covenantal marker of Christian identity – not whiteness. And far from leading to a new kind of tribalism, recovering a theology of Israel joins us to the activist faith of Jesus the Jew. And so Jennings encourages us to engage deeply and thoughtfully on:

> The racialized bodies of blacks and Jews in modernity. Such a meditation would allow us to peer through the cracks of modern racial calculus and discern fragments of the original situation of Israel and gentiles, of Israel and a gentile church, of the Jewish body and the gentile body joined.[6]

As an Anglican it seems vital not simply to recognize our toxic history of power relations with respect to our colonial history, but also to other religious traditions. Of course, many Christian denominations, particularly predominantly non-white traditions, without the legacy of this history often have a far healthier and joyful approach to evangelism.

For every Christian the whole reason and praxis for our evangelism flows out of God's desire to bring all into relationship with God. In Christ, God elects to be the Saviour of all people. Indeed, Christ is the only possible means of redemption being possible for anyone. If this is not held to, then Christianity simply becomes one among many religions, each of which share certain characteristics amid their differences. However, all the ground on which we stand is reliant upon the particularity of the person and work of God in Christ – which the gospel holds out as *the* way, not simply one of the ways, that God is known. Yet this God is at work in all people, drawing them in with grace. This is the true and living God who made the world and everything in it.

God is not a 'thing', one of a type of genus, one particular example of a category. In witness we are not attesting to a product or commodity. We are not presenting a 'better product'.

Many adherents of other religious traditions find solace, peace and comfort in their religion. We too often assume everyone who is not a Christian is benighted and unhappy. Worse still, we fall into the trap of approaching conversations with the idea that until we arrive and open our mouths, God has been absent. What should our starting point be?

We are talking of one of whom Aquinas said no greater can be conceived. This God is the creator of all, one who chooses to love all and know all. There is nothing and no one that is hidden from him. The work of the Holy Spirit is to apply the work done for all in Christ, to bring people in on it, as it were. Through the Spirit, God is at work redemptively in other faiths, which clearly know and cherish God's presence.

Some follow the German Jesuit priest Karl Rahner, who in the middle of the last century coined the term 'anonymous Christian' for one who lives in the state of grace through faith, hope and love, yet who has no explicit knowledge of the fact that his life is orientated in grace-given salvation to Jesus Christ. It was not that every adherent of other faiths be considered in this way, but 'every human being is really and truly exposed to the influence of divine supernatural grace, which offers an interior union with God.'[7] Something similar is found in the theology of C. S. Lewis, which he sets out in *The Last Battle*. At the end of the world and beginning of the next, Aslan meets one of Tash's servants, who has spent his life denying and defying Aslan, but is told, 'Child, all the service thou hast done to Tash, I account as service done to me.'[8] The trouble with this line of 'anonymous' service and devotion, done seemingly for one but counted for another, is that it betrays a patronizing and colonizing presumption and understandably can cause deep offence to members of other faiths.

C. S. Lewis and many others have held to an encounter between Christ and those of other faiths after death. Yale's Professor George Lindbeck talked about this post-mortem evangelization as the only way of making sense of the claims of the Christian faith to the universal work of Christ. Some find:

YEARNING FOR THE VAST AND ENDLESS SEA

... a hint within the Canon of scripture, puzzling indeed and obscure yet at the same time reassuringly restrained, that the mysterious interval between Good Friday afternoon and Easter morning was not empty of significance, but that in it too Jesus Christ was active as the saviour of the world. It is a hint, too, surely, that those who in subsequent ages have died without ever having had a real chance to believe in Christ are not outside the scope of his mercy and will not perish eternally without being given in the same way that is beyond our knowledge an opportunity to hear the gospel and accept him as their saviour.[9]

There are those of course who point out that, apart from 1 Peter 3.19, scripture does not hold out a strong basis for belief that we are judged on anything other than our response to the gifts given during our earthly life. However, in this as in all things, in all our debating and pronouncing we should find comfort and encouragement that our understandings are incredibly limited, our perspectives particularly partial, and that what we believe doesn't make it true. Our task is simply to seek humbly to make sense of the things that have been given. In fact, the followers of Jesus would do well to do as Jesus did, when asked to give a clear ruling as to who was in and who was out. Instead, Jesus rather raises the stakes by opening up our imagination to a banquet where 'people will come from east and west, from north and south, and will eat in the kingdom of God. Indeed, some are last who will be first, and some are first who will be last' (Luke 13.29–30). This is a matter for God alone. Our position as Christians doesn't give us an entitlement to know or deduce God's final judgement on other people. Only God can answer certain questions.

Any ideological attitude that draws a straight line between religious practices and habits as the basis for the reception of the benefits of the work of Christ can too easily open the door to salvation gifted on the basis of something other than grace. Simply to praise goodness and religious practice in other faiths

WHO IS THE GOSPEL FOR?

needs to bear in mind Lesslie Newbigin's cautionary comment that 'it is precisely at the point of the highest ethical and spiritual achievement that the religions find themselves threatened by and therefore ranged against the gospel'.[10] Salvation is not appropriated through religious observance. It is not achieved by human effort, even if that effort is pious.

We bring only the confession of our sin and our need for mercy and forgiveness. We are met not in our strength, but in our weakness; not in our holiness, but in our wrongdoing; not as those who are moral, but as those who are immoral. We are met in our need for mercy and grace; and the key 'ingredient' in it all is faith. Faith not as an achievement of the person, or displayed in sacred devotion, but faith in the one from whom we need to receive mercy, on whose grace we ultimately rely. It is not a need for knowledge, as if our standing before the God who created us were reliant upon our being on the receiving end of information.

Faith is a gift of grace that is enabled entirely by the Holy Spirit. The Spirit opens the door for humans to respond to whatever revelation God has given to them. Indeed, the Roman Catholic theologian Hans Urs von Balthasar talks of the 'cruciform' shape of grace: a grace that acknowledges the essential connection between grace and Christ and the meeting place in a life being an awareness of the need for mercy. For we cannot go behind Calvary to argue our way to a conclusion that would make the cross meaningless or not essential:

> The revelation of God's saving love and power in Jesus entitles and requires me to believe that God purposes the salvation of all ... But it does not entitle me to believe that this purpose is accomplished in any way which ignores or bypasses the historical event by which it was in fact revealed and effected.[11]

But what if the shape of this gracious mercy can be traced through cruciform patterns that, at their core, evidence a recognition of the need for mercy, forgiveness, kindness and undeserved blessing, which the Spirit is constantly working to open up in life after life? In such a way, Max Warren talks of the 'unknown Christ' who saves even when unrecognized as the Saviour. What if rather than siding with Karl Rahner's rather clunky 'anonymous Christian' idea we heed Vatican II's theme of all people finding 'fulfilment in Christ'? In other words, discerning yearnings and echoes in religions and spiritual practices that find their fulfilment in Christ. It was Jesus himself who stated, 'I have other sheep that do not belong to this fold. I must bring them also, and they will listen to my voice. So there will be one flock, one shepherd' (John 10.16). After all, Jesus said that when he was lifted up from the earth, 'I ... will draw all people to myself' (John 12.32).

> What all this means for the ultimate relationship to God as father is mostly a mystery. We have no overview of it, no time-scale for it, just glimpses of it from time to time, and these can come through people of all religions and none, and through experiences labeled 'religious' or not. Jesus is free to relate to all in both open and hidden ways.[12]

Our stance must be openness, inquisitiveness and humility – characterized by risk and an expectation that we will be surprised. To interact truly and enquiringly demands this risk of faith; this is our faithful witness to Christ. There is an essential listening and learning, discerning and discovering the cruciform pattern of the Spirit's work. And, as this begins, there is little for the Western Christian to say in the world forum of faiths except *nostra culpa; nostra maxima culpa* ('our most grievous fault').[13] We must, in Max Warren's powerful picture, begin by taking our shoes off, for the ground we are standing on is holy.

But meet and listen, engage and talk, we must. The church has for too long buried its treasure in the ground. As Christians we go to meet our neighbour on the basis of our commitment to Jesus Christ. In all of our engagement we follow his example: always meeting others with generosity and grace. We follow his example by asking questions and being utterly committed to the other. Our witness to those of other faiths is part of our obedience to Christ, compelled by God's great love which is for all. In recent years much has been done through presence and engagement to build up trust, honesty and understanding. For example, the Christian Muslim Forum has agreed guidelines for witness that lay the groundwork for sharing faith.[14] These guidelines are remarkable for what they say and indicate about power relations, naming as unacceptable anything that is coercive, manipulative or offering material inducements. It recognizes each person should have the freedom to change their mind. The shared ground here is because Muslims are also committed to witness (*Da'wah*) and seeing conversions. It must be noted that some other religious traditions find it fundamentally problematic; most particularly, I reflect on a painful conversation with a Hindu acquaintance who took my desire for him to consider Jesus as a threat to destroy his culture, and Chief Rabbi Ephraim Mirvis's afterword to *God's Unfailing Word* in which he reflects honestly on the Jewish community's existential terror of evangelism.[15]

Along with the apostle John, every Christian looks forward to the time in God's future when we will see 'a great multitude that no one could count, from every nation, from all tribes and peoples and languages, standing before the throne and before the Lamb' (Revelation 7.9).

This will be the work of God, the coming of whose kingdom is guaranteed and whose will cannot, and will not, be thwarted:

O the depth of the riches and wisdom and knowledge of God! How unsearchable are his judgements and how inscrutable his ways!

'For who has known the mind of the Lord?
   Or who has been his counsellor?'
'Or who has given a gift to him,
   to receive a gift in return?'

For from him and through him and to him are all things. To him be the glory for ever. Amen. (Romans 11.33–36)

All knowing, all powerful and all loving God,
Whose ways are perfect, whose heart is kind, whose mercy is
*   unceasing,*
You freely choose to make our redemption your will.
How great are your ways that you desire all you have made
*   to be saved and come to know the truth.*
Forgive us for being too easily misled to suppose your divine
*   freedom threatens our human freedom. We acknowledge*
*   we can only be free when we bow to your ways and*
*   means.*
We thank you for your 'no' to us which liberates us and your
*   'yes' to us which saves us.*
By your Spirit renew in each of us the sense of the gift of our
*   chosenness, that we might tell those who have excluded*
*   themselves of your choice for them in Christ.*
You are the one who knows all people, nations and cultures.
*   We believe no one is outside of your will or your mercy.*
Stir in your church Christ-like ways of listening, questioning,
*   meeting, speaking and loving. By your Spirit inhabit the*
*   spaces between us, and may we discern you in all your*
*   ways.*
Fill us with hope and anticipation of that gathering with
*   multitudes that no one can count, from every nation, tribe*
*   and people and language before your throne. Amen.*

Notes

1 David Ford, 2021, *The Gospel of John: A Theological Commentary*, Grand Rapids, MI: Baker Academic, p. 20.

2 Willie Jennings, 2017, *Acts: A Theological Commentary on the Bible*, Louisville, KY: Westminster John Knox Press, p. 93.

3 Lesslie Newbigin, 1995, *The Open Secret: An Introduction to the Theology of Mission*, New York: Eerdmans, pp. 78–9.

4 Newbigin, *The Open Secret*, p. 216.

5 For example, Newbigin, C. of E. resources, D'Costa, Miroslav Volf, Pinnock.

6 Willie Jennings, 2011, *The Christian Imagination: Theology and the Origins of Race*, New Haven, CT: Yale University Press, p. 275.

7 Karl Rahner, 1961, *Theological Investigations*, Vol. 14, Baltimore, MD: Helicon Press, p. 283.

8 C. S. Lewis, 1980, *The Last Battle*, London: Fontana Lions, p. 155.

9 N. Cranfield, 1984, quoted in George Lindbeck, *The Nature of Doctrine: Religion and Theology in a Postliberal Age*, Philadelphia, PA: Westminster John Knox Press, p. 189.

10 Lesslie Newbigin, 2014, *The Gospel in a Pluralistic Society*, London: SPCK, p. 193.

11 Newbigin, *The Gospel in a Pluralistic Society*, p. 200.

12 Ford, *The Gospel of John*, pp. 279–80.

13 Newbigin, *The Gospel in a Pluralistic Society*, p. 137.

14 The statement begins, 2009, 'As members of the Christian Muslim Forum we are deeply committed to our own faiths [Christianity and Islam] and wish to bear witness to them. Under the aegis of the Christian Muslim Forum, at a meeting held on 24 June 2009, a set of Ethical Guidelines were agreed and offered to the wider church for implementation. The following is offered to help equip Christians and Muslims in sharing their faith with integrity and compassion for those they meet.

  1 We bear witness to, and proclaim, our faith not only through words but though our attitudes, actions and lifestyles.

  2 We cannot convert people, only God can do that. In our language and methods we should recognize that people's choice of faith is primarily a matter between themselves and God.

  3 Sharing our faith should never be coercive; this is especially important when working with children, young people and vulnerable adults. Everyone should have the choice to accept or reject the message we proclaim and we will accept people's choices without resentment.

  4 Whilst we might care for people in need or who are facing personal crises, we should never manipulate these situations in order to gain a convert.

  5 An invitation to convert should never be linked with financial, material or other inducements. It should be a decision of the heart and mind alone.

  6 We will speak of our faith without demeaning or ridiculing the faith of others.

7 We will speak clearly and honestly about our faith, even when that is uncomfortable or controversial.

8 We will be honest about our motivations for activities and we will inform people when events will include the sharing of faith.

9 Whilst recognizing that either community will naturally rejoice with and support those who have chosen to join them, we will be sensitive to the loss that others may feel.

10 Whilst we may feel hurt when someone we know and love chooses to leave our faith, we will respect their decision and will not force them to stay or harass them afterwards.'

15 The Faith and Order Commission, 2019, *God's Unfailing Word: Theological and Practical Perspectives on Christian–Jewish Relations*, London: Church House Publishing.

7

Why Evangelism?

Is it a surprise that when the general tenet of existence is survival of the fittest, the very reason to exist becomes merely survival? It's true for many of us – we cling to our youth by our false fingertips and attempt to keep decay at bay by banishing our grey hairs. It's true for us commercially – the demographic of the emptying high street means the only question for retail outlets is how they can survive the next year. The right to survive might be nobody's, but the motivation to survive is everybody's, and the attempt to survive has quickly and genuinely become, literally, our *raison d'être*.

In such a scheme of things the church of Jesus Christ in the Western world is facing the starkest challenge – as the increasingly disinterested and baffled world assumes churches will have become museums within a generation. And of course the stats affirm the backstory, which suggests that survival is far from certain. Many Christians take it upon themselves to hold our 'feet to the fire' and face us with a grim reality of the church's certain passing, unless something happens, and happens quick. We are awash with the well-meaning suggestions that flow in – rebranding, upgrading, streamlining, modernizing, updating – all to achieve the ubiquitous end of 'becoming relevant'. All we should take with us from this point are those things that are going to give us the surest chance of survival.

So is evangelism about survival? Is it our means of securing the future of the church?

Most months, without even listening out for it, you can hear someone say, with great urgency, 'The church is just a generation away from extinction.' In its slipstream this lifeboat – because it is said as part of a rescue attempt – is followed by the anxiety that unless we do something effective and decisive the future for the Christian faith is in doubt. This 'rescue' must ensure we pass on the baton to the next generation to guarantee the continuation of right believing and behaving, practising and performing; evangelism is the means of securing the future. In another slipstream is the desire to move the Christian faith from the margins to a place of greater visibility and influence, for dwindling numbers make it hard to argue for a prominent place at the broadcasting microphone or the benches of power.

The solution to the above is simple and urgent: do something fast – make more Christians! Evangelism quickly becomes a scheme for survival, or a church growth strategy. But that Old Testament prophet of a theologian, Walter Brueggemann, cautions against this:

> Evangelism is never aimed at institutional enhancement or aggrandisement. It is aimed simply and solely at summoning people to new, liberated obedience to the governor of all created reality.[1]

The church will grow as, in the language of Brueggemann, more and more people switch allegiance, a new loyalty that is signalled publicly by baptism. There is nothing quite like the joy and encouragement this new life brings to a church. But as much as we want the church to grow, to be alive, to be full, this is not the motive for evangelism; instead it is its consequence.

At other times the motive for evangelism has been to produce more people like us; to replicate Christians. Often this has emerged from the unhealthy practice of power, racism and more than a whiff of superiority. Suffice to say that the history of the *Why* of evangelism is played in the key of fear, control and ignorance.

Survival of the person being evangelized is also a driver. In his book *The Divine Conspiracy*, Dallas Willard articulates how, for many, the main motivation for evangelism is the effort and imperative to change people's eternal destiny. Willard uses a powerful analogy: imagine the soul of every person who has ever lived can be read like a barcode.[2] At the day of judgement every barcode will be read by the divine scanner. If the soul belongs to one who has prayed the 'sinner's prayer' – a prayer usually shorter than 100 words in which a person admits they are a sinner, believes that Jesus died for their sins, confesses their sin and repents, and then decides to follow Jesus – then the scanner will always beep 'SAVED'. Because the belief is that all that is needed is for the person to pray a prayer, it has too often been the end that all evangelism is driven towards and assessed by.

Dallas Willard's point is actually not so much about evangelism, it is more about discipleship. His question is whether just getting people to a particular point or over a line, by whatever means necessary or possible, is true to all that Jesus taught. (Willard says it isn't.) But I have always found it helpful to think about this in evangelism. For a large number of people, techniques in play in evangelism betray this mindset – that of the essential, literally do-or-die requirement to secure the praying of a prayer of decision that will for all time alter the eternal destination of that person's soul. I have been present when it hasn't seemed to matter that those praying along with the prayer a phrase at a time didn't really know what was being offered to them, or anything of the implications of being a disciple of the living Lord. What mattered was that salvation was now theirs because at one point in their lives, with whatever meaning or motive, this person 'prayed the prayer'.

Now of course it is not that there is no such thing as conversion. It is not that for some people a moment of decision can't be rapid, or seemingly coming out of the blue and taking everyone by surprise. Rather, it is that not only are some of the motives and techniques at best a most disturbing caricature of the gospel, the drive of salvaging souls from hell is also not a *primary* motive for evangelism in the scriptures. Fear isn't the driver of the good news. Bishop Lesslie Newbigin carefully states that as he addresses the motive for evangelism:

I am not placing at the centre of the argument the question of the salvation or perdition of the individual. Clearly that is part of what is involved, but my contention is that the biblical picture is distorted if this is put at the centre.[3]

I would argue therefore that fear for future souls should not be the main motivation of our proclamation of the good news. From everything I can understand, St Paul patently didn't assume everyone's salvation was in his hands. How else would he have been able to tell the Christians in Rome that he has 'fully proclaimed the good news of Christ' (Romans 15.19) in the vast geographical area from Jerusalem to the Adriatic, and there is 'no further place for me in these regions' (Romans 15.23)? His motive in evangelism was urgently to participate in the work of God to awaken people to what God has done for them in Christ. But it is difficult to conclude that his primary motive was the weight of knowing that every single person's personal eternal destiny was his responsibility.

The American author Annie Dillard narrates an encounter that puts this starkly:

An Inuit hunter asked the local missionary priest: 'If I did not know about God and sin, would I go to hell?'
'No,' said the priest, 'not if you did not know.'
'Then why,' asked the Inuit earnestly, 'did you tell me?'[4]

This isn't a book about eschatology or the future destination of men and women. But because it is about evangelism the question of salvation isn't *not* relevant, though my sense is that Newbigin is right to decouple it from the primary motive for evangelism. Of course, the question about receiving the gift of salvation is the question of life; as Dietrich Bonhoeffer said: 'The enquiry about salvation is the only ultimate serious question in the world. But it isn't easy to formulate it in the right terms.'[5]

It isn't, to my mind at least, that the gospel doesn't summon men and women to repent and take hold of the life that God has made possible in Christ. It isn't that those living apart from

Christ don't need to be alerted to the consequences of choosing to live apart from God. It isn't that all will be saved. But it is that the announcement of the events that have changed the world and the one who brought these events about isn't to be grasped because of what there is to be feared, but for what there is to be received. The driver isn't our personal gain. The driver is God.

> Therefore, knowing the fear of the Lord, we try to persuade others ... For the love of Christ urges us on, because we are convinced that one has died for all; therefore all have died. And he died for all, so that those who live might live no longer for themselves, but for him who died and was raised for them. (2 Corinthians 5.11, 14–15)

The *Why* of evangelism isn't our own survival or even the ultimate survival of those we are trying to persuade – because, of course, we are not neutral about the response. But the reason why we must share this, why we are compelled, convinced and constrained, is because of the goodness of the love of God. Because this love has come to make all the difference. And we cannot bear people living a moment longer without knowing this. In fact, this is the vocation we have been charged with; we are entrusted with the message of reconciliation, those through whom God makes a personal appeal.

It is relationship that is the driver; not enemies but friends, no longer strangers but sons and daughters. All this is a gift from God. A gift made not just possible but actual by God's work in Christ Jesus.

In Christ we are recipients of grace and mercy, unflinching commitment and loving-kindness. We are the adopted members of the family of God, named as his people and his beloved friends. In Christ we have been set free from the slavery of sin and declared to be the objects of his liberating action. Our pasts have been redeemed and our futures have been guaranteed. In Christ we are chosen, forgiven, accepted and cherished. Our judgement has been enacted on Jesus Christ and we have, incomprehensibly, nothing to fear. The one through whom all things were made has given us life by dying our death and rising to new life. Everything has changed because of what our God has done for us. No longer at enmity with God, no longer divided from one another, we have been remade. And this is not just true for us, but the whole world. We have more to look forward to than we can take in. How can we keep from singing?

The *Why* of evangelism is for people to come into relationship with God, not for what they might receive, but for the sake of the God that gives it all. Writers of Christian spirituality have never been able to completely separate out the benefits of the gospel – what we receive from God – from loving God. It is the undertaking of a lifetime, of all of our worship, service and discipleship. It is the theme at the heart of the book of Job – that, rather than suffering itself. In this story from the heart of the Jewish wisdom tradition, the question is whether Job loves God for everything that he has been given or whether he loves God for God's own sake. For does anyone truly love God for God's own sake? In the story everything is taken away from Job – because the Accuser is convinced that left with nothing, Job will turn round and curse God. But as Job sits distraught and devastated in dust and ashes, having lost everything, he refuses to curse God. We are let in on the struggle of it, the mystery of it, but we witness one who actually loves God for God's sake.

It was a constant theme for that astonishing Jesuit priest Francis Xavier, whose life would never be the same after he encountered Ignatius of Loyola at the University of Paris. Whose life is after encountering Ignatius? Xavier was one of Loyola's first extraordinary nine converts. Xavier left for India in 1541, and visited many places in the Far East with cross in hand. He wrote this hymn:

> My God, I love Thee; not because I hope for heav'n thereby,
> nor yet for fear that loving not I might forever die;
> but for that Thou didst all mankind upon the cross embrace;
> for us didst bear the nails and spear, and manifold disgrace;

And griefs and torments numberless, and sweat of agony;
e'en death itself, and all for man, who was Thine enemy.
Then why, most loving Jesus Christ, should I not love
    Thee well?
Not for the sake of winning heav'n, nor any fear of hell;

Not with the hope of gaining aught, nor seeking a reward,
but as Thyself hast loved me, O ever loving Lord!
E'en so I love Thee, and will love, and in Thy praise will sing,
solely because Thou art my God and my eternal King!

We can never grasp the depths and heights of what has been given to us in Christ. Why has God done this for us? For what purpose? For what end?

For God's own sake – for the sake of God's love.

Not only is it not about the survival of the individual, my belief is that it is not about the survival and self-preservation of the church either.

It is my firmest conviction that evangelism is essential to the being and work of the church, but not for its survival. And while we're at it, evangelism and witness isn't just one thing the church should do, one department/committee/team every church should have, one thing among many the church should be committed to. It is everything the church is and does. But the church's calling is not to ensure its own survival, significance or status. We are not living for popularity, power or prestige. The church's primary – in fact *only* – vocation is *to be* the church.

But as everyone's favourite fictional US President, Jed Bartlet in the series *The West Wing*, would then ask, 'What are the next ten words?' It is about the complexity of an answer, not the slogan. 'Yes' to the big headline, the sweeping, encapsulating declaration of fact. But what are we talking about in the statement 'the church is called to be the church'?

Like children on Christmas Day who want to unwrap all the presents quickly, we want everything that is ours to be separated from the reasons why it has been given. After all, it's given freely, isn't it? And of course the answer is, 'Yes, it is given freely.' But *why* is it given? Jesus Christ did not take flesh, suffer, die and rise to life for our own personal and private blessing.

The reason we are called is not that we might be set apart for our own sakes, but that we are those through whom the call goes out to others. The reason the light has shone on us is not simply to illuminate our lives, or top up our tan, but that we bear the light to all in darkness. The reason we are the recipients of the gift of grace is not that we might bask in its benefits, but that we will bear the gifts of grace to all. The reason we are the objects of God's extravagant blessing is not to keep it to ourselves, but so that we will be conduits of that blessing to the whole world. The purpose of God's saving work for, in, on, with and to us is that we might bear faithful witness to him. What is the church for? The church is for God. And because of who this God is, and what this God has done, the church is for the world.

This continually makes and remakes the church. The good news forms and reforms us, and not just on the day of Pentecost or in the pages of the Acts of the Apostles. We are continually remade, not just in a handful of watershed moments in history, but in *every* moment. We are always being converted by the gospel; and that to which we owe everything determines everything.

Of course, this has not been our history. Our earliest records – the letters of Paul, Peter, John – give unambiguous evidence of how our brokenness gets in the way. We recognize our propensity, even compulsion, to reduce the gospel by taking away and then adding, so as to make faith the vehicle for our own desires and ambitions. We are used to cutting and pasting, shaping and editing the gospel to our world view. The church of Jesus Christ has continually set and fallen into every trap and at every hurdle. Recently, Lambeth Palace Library hosted an exhibition called 'Enslavement: Voices from the Archives'. It was shocking – particularly the so-called 'Slave' Bible from 1808 in Haiti. It is the most startling example of reducing the gospel for the ends of retaining power. Whereas a standard Bible has 1,189 chapters, this Haiti version has only 232. It excludes 90 per cent of the Old Testament and 50 per cent of the New Testament – Exodus only starts at chapter 19 – and every mention of God releasing his people from slavery is deleted.

Our history is littered with disasters of the good news of Christ Jesus being co-opted to serve sinful systems of power, greed, dominion, control and comfort, whether this is the so-called conversion of Constantine – not converted enough if you ask me – making Christianity the religion of the state; bloodshed in the name of the prince of peace; or capture and enslavement in the name of social order.

As the gospel takes flesh in a community in a particular place at a particular time, unwittingly we slip into cultural assumptions, tastes, aspirations and pitfalls. Of course, there is no such thing as a church that isn't embedded in a particular culture, but we can be so blind that we can't see how the church can look far too much like everything else in this culture rather than Jesus Christ. We are often obsessed with celebrity, image, comfort, money, reputation and influence – not to mention male-dominated, white and homophobic. The Western church has conflated Christian faith with the wider culture to devastating effect. It is a toxic mix. Reductionism trivializes, undermines, violates and blasphemes God.

But is this compromise bound to happen because of the systems and structures we've put in place? Doesn't this call us all to be anti-establishment, anti-institution, non-conformists? While it might get baked in by institutionalization, it is not necessarily caused by it. In recent history some of the renewing movements in the church have quickly taken up arms against anything that looks vaguely established. Everything is denounced apart from the present. Everyone else is an obstacle except those who subscribe to this particular point of view. Such simplistic and binary ways of assessing the situation offer us no long-term help.

Andy Root, a thinker whose wisdom is a rich gift to the church, tells the story of an encounter with a young man whose reputation as a radical, passionate, committed all-out-for-Jesus disciple went ahead of him. He was sought out by a famous Bible scholar who wanted to talk to him about faith. The topic of belonging to a worshipping community came up:

> The young man explained that he rarely went, telling the professor unfortunately Sunday worship was just too boring.
> 'I thought you loved Jesus,' the professor asked.
> 'I do,' the young man returned with genuine intensity. 'I really do!'
> 'So,' the professor asked, 'do you think you'd be willing to die for Jesus?'
> Now more reserved, the young man said, 'Yes ... yes, I think I would. I would die for Jesus.'
> 'So, let me get this straight,' the professor continued, 'You're willing to die for Jesus, but not be bored for Jesus?'[6]

We must hold the complexity of it all. It is not the necessity of institutions that are, per se, the problem; although the Lord constantly holds the plumbline up against his church, judgement begins with the house of God. And of course the prophets who are raised up to bring that corrective admonition are nearly always those from the margins. Every church structure, every church organization, institution and establishment, must bear faithful witness to the one whose name we bear. And it must not, and cannot, be assumed that because particular patterns of governance, authority and methods have served effectively in the past, they still provide the right framework for the present and the future. Diverse and differing organizational forms of church are biblically and historically valid.

We witness that propensity time and again in the people of God, throughout scripture, to take the calling and blessing of God and turn it into a thing for their own ends. Why else would Jesus' strongest words of rebuke and judgement be spoken to religious leaders: 'For you have taken away the key of knowledge; you did not enter yourselves, and you hindered those who were entering' (Luke 11.52).

There is hope, but it is not found in initiatives, reviews or modernization. It is found as we insist on letting the gospel define our everything. What are we willing to let the gospel do?

The gospel comes to us to make us witnesses. It's undeniable there are times when we have spoken and acted as if the gospel has come to bring civil religion, clericalism, individualization, happiness, authenticity, behaviour management and progress. The gospel has been reduced to some general, but praiseworthy, values and principles. And it happens quietly and subtly, under the radar, almost as a seemingly obvious – even if well-meaning – evolution, which we don't even notice at the time. The fire that burns petrifies and the living water that flowed becomes stagnant.

We could call all sorts of witnesses, open another couple of bottles of wine, and diagnose all the church's terrible shortcomings and offences. But living in constant review and critique isn't life-giving for anyone. As Professor Miroslav Volf says, 'To change the world, we need an "I have a dream" speech, not an "I have a complaint speech".'[7]

It is the dream of the gospel that gives us somewhere to stand and something to say. In fact, it is only the gospel that can lead us out of here. It is only because of the gospel that we can, that we must, have hope. In what way does the gospel transform the church? In every way!

While the church is brought into being by Jesus Christ, he is, of course, apart from the church. While there is much that could be diagnosed from a psychological, organizational, societal and financial perspective about the church, none of those things go to the root of our greatest need. Without a doubt, our most serious, pressing and basic requirement is theological. It is to encounter Jesus Christ.

That most quoted of New Testament verses is addressed not to individuals, but to the whole of the church at Laodicea:

'Listen! I am standing at the door, knocking; if you hear my voice and open the door, I will come in to you and eat with you, and you with me' (Revelation 3.20). What a profound picture – Jesus knocking on the door of the church. The Word of God speaks, that we might heed the words of life and respond, that today we would hear his voice, that we, the thirsty and hungry would come to the one who desires to give us all we need.

We are urged by the Lord in Isaiah: 'listen, so that you may live' (Isaiah 55.3).

This is addressed not primarily to individuals, but to God's people as a body.

Because even though the gospel is directed to every person personally, it is essentially a corporate remaking. By the animating Holy Spirit, God makes us part of the body of Christ. Each person has an essential role in the body. It is not just like a team that needs lots of different skills and positional players. It is not just like an orchestra, which has those wonderful instruments that, played together, make profound music. It is not merely a functional 'We're better together' thing. It is because we find ourselves in the corporate identity and vocation of this body.

Often we are so functional that our participation in a local church community is regulated simply by our own determination. It comes down to what works for us. This means, more than in any other generation, we have swathes of churchless Christians. Yes, there is often a desperate story behind each one, but the determining decision around church seems to be what best fits with me. We have become curators of our own faith, self-appointed experts in knowing where to go to get what we want – all enabled and encouraged by offerings made freely available to us from across the world with the ease of a double-click.

Is it possible to be a Christian and not be part of a church? Yes, of course. But that's not a very good question. It puts *us* at the centre once again. Can the church fully realize its vocation without every Christian? No, it can't. Every withdrawal in the church impacts the power of our corporate witness. It is not about us – our preferences and inclinations, our own convictions and personal loyalties – it is about Christ and it is about others. Our failure to take our place impacts the viability of our witness.

What if the formative question around church isn't 'What is going to give me what I want?' or 'What do I think I need?' but 'To whom is the Spirit calling me to belong for the sake of what Christ is doing?' Because it will always be somewhere – a certain place. With some others – certain people.

Somewhere

To be for the world, we need to have a strong and coherent understanding of our being part of the world. Our part, place and presence in the world is determined by theology, not by economics, ergonomics or market forces. To witness to Jesus Christ, the eternal logos made flesh, the Holy Spirit brings about the birth of his body in a particular place, at a particular time, among a particular people. The gospel is lived by incarnational witness, an embodied community. A local congregation is the basic unit of Christian witness.[8] This calls for a profound awareness and openness to the people who are in the places where we are 'set'.

Consider church planting – one of the most effective forms of evangelism. Professor Stefan Paas sets up a defining metaphor.[9] Imagine a golf course in a country such as Dubai. The golf course exists because it is transplanted into an area and so has to be maintained artificially. The soil will be imported, the grass will be laid or sown, the cultivation of the square miles of the course will have to be continually supported, upheld and preserved by outside stimuli – it will have to be constantly watered, irrigated and preserved. Take any of the props away and the whole thing will go to seed in days. It is only alive because it receives the external support. It is only sustainable as long as the unnatural conditions are maintained. It is not really viable in the long term. Nor is it authentic to the place where it is located. If it were to be viable in the long term, if it were to be sensible to its surroundings, it would have to begin in a completely different way – with the conditions that were natural to it.

The problem with imported models of church planting is not simply that they are only really sustainable as long as the exterior props are guaranteed, it is a theological problem – it seems to pay little heed to the particularity of the area and its people. Each local church looks, sounds, engages, serves and works in a particular way because of where it is located. Church holds particularity in high esteem – what God is doing in one place is unique, and while it's likely it will share similarities and patterns, we are not mere carbon copies.

Encountering others

Being in church with others isn't easy. There are no ideals. It takes place in real time among us. Scripture again and again merges the reception of the good news with lives that exemplify it. St Paul exhorts the Philippians to 'live your life in a manner worthy of the gospel of Christ' (Philippians 1.27).

The gospel makes a people and requires those people to live as good news for one another. It is a profoundly interactive encounter, not just the repetition of past practices. The Christian community practises the virtues of Christ by the enabling and empowering of the Holy Spirit. This is a community where the life of Christ should characterise every encounter – where humility, dignity, goodness, honesty, joy, patience, resilience, willingness to suffer for one another, truth, grace, empathy and love, love, love determine the spaces between us. The assumptions that people – younger generations especially – have about the church will only be addressed by our lives.

One of the most profound practices that bears faithful witness to the gospel is how we handle disagreement in a way that

witnesses to Christ. Each struggle is an occasion for the continuing conversion of the church, as those who might – apart from
Christ – consider one another to be enemies commit instead to
relating only to one another as to Christ. Paul addresses this
to the church in Rome. In chapter 14 he speaks of two big
fall-out issues: observation of holy days, and buying and eating
food from the local market that has been sacrificed to idols.
On both these issues, Paul has very strong views. Yet he refuses
to side with either party, because his governing concern is the
witness of the church. The way they are dividing on these issues
is causing unfaithful witness to Christ – for such people are
judging one another and making assumptions on the standing
of each other before Christ. But as only God is judge, and each
person stands before Christ, this is compromising their witness.
So he calls them, despite deeply held and argued convictions, to
pursue what makes for peace and life together. The power of
Christian witness amid disagreement is beyond telling – for it is
utterly counter-cultural; the society we're part of divides, hates
and excludes those with whom it disagrees. Christians unite,
love and include one another.

Of course, anyone who has been part of a Christian community knows there is nothing harder than living out the love
and grace of Jesus. Sometimes we experience seasons of excruciating relational breakdown, when it is clear that the integrity
of the community's witness is highly compromised. And while
it might cause us now to take a moment to pray for the communities that have been so wounded by disunity, it actually
causes us to underline in permanent Sharpie that how we dis-
agree is indeed both the most powerful and most undermining
form of our witness.

It is in loving one another that the Christian community practises the news that the world has little comprehension of how
to hear or enact. The message of love, grace and forgiveness
might be initially welcomed, but it will also cause dissension. I
remember leading a memorial service for a community that had
been devastated by a fatal attack on three of its members. The

bishop present raised the necessity of forgiveness for the per-petrator. The gathered congregation bristled and some walked out incensed. But if the good news doesn't challenge and reset our patterns of unforgiveness, revenge and hatred, nothing else will. It's not just good advice, good suggestions, good recom-mendations, good ideals or good counsel. It's good news. We won't hear it anywhere else, or see it lived apart from Christ.

Insisting that the *Why* for evangelism isn't for the survival of the individual or the church, but for the sake of God and being faithful witnesses, leaves us with one final place to stand.

Why do we proclaim and witness? Lesslie Newbigin gently introduces the defining reason, and it was a revelation to me when I started to think about it. The night before Jesus died, he said, 'where I am, there will my servant be also' (John 12.26). We who have been loved and called by the Lord will want to be where Christ is:

> And where he is is on the frontier which runs between the kingdom of God and the usurped power of the evil one; there is no other way to be with him. At the heart of mission is simply the desire to be with him and give him the service of our lives.[10]

The gospel that remakes the church remakes it in order that it might be with Jesus in God's continuing work to establish the kingdom. The aim of church isn't more church. It is for the glory of the King and the service of God's kingdom. Each day a billion Christians will pray for the coming of the kingdom, not for the expansion of the church.

We are where God is as we proclaim and serve, when we feed the hungry, give a drink to the thirsty, welcome in the stranger, clothe the naked, take care of the sick, visit those in prison. That's Jesus' own list from Matthew 25. The Holy Spirit, through the life of Jesus, animates us to do this. For in the same way that the kingdom is partial reality while anticipating future completion, so the Holy Spirit is given in part now in anticipation of experiencing the fullness of God's presence. The Spirit is the 'down-payment', the guarantee of what is to come. The presence of God is 'already and not yet', just as the kingdom of God is 'already and not yet'.

Of course, these go hand in glove. The Spirit is sent by the Father to create the conditions of the kingdom. After the resurrection, Jesus showed the disciples his hands and his side. They rejoiced. This is how much they were loved by him. Then he breathed on them, '"As the Father has sent me, so I send you." When he had said this, he breathed on them and said to them, "Receive the Holy Spirit"' (John 20.21–22). Why is it that we tend to reduce the work and influence of the Spirit to within the walls of the church? Pope Francis revisits the Revelation 3 quote that tells the church that Jesus is knocking on the door; but rather than knocking to be let in, he is knocking to be let out. If the already-and-not-yet Spirit comes to bring about the already-and-not-yet kingdom of God, why do we have such limited imagination as to what the gift of the Holy Spirit might do for the church, which exists not for its own survival but to serve Jesus in the constant establishment of the promised kingdom of God?

The reason we invite all people to respond to God's never-ending, unquenchable, stronger-than-death love is because this is what Jesus did. And what he is still doing. And where else would we want to be? And what else would we want to do?

Yahweh, Lord Almighty,
The One who was, and is, and is to come,
May we love you not for the benefits we receive from you,
But for your own sake, because you are worthy of all praise.
How can we keep from singing?
May it be your love that compels us, your kindness that
ignites us and your renown that inspires us.
By your Spirit flood us once again with the joy of our
inheritance in Christ.

May we realize who we have been made, called and
empowered to be as we join you in your work to summon
all creation to find fulfilment in your Son Christ Jesus.
Join our voices together in the beauty and harmony that
anticipates and echoes the melody of heaven,
And bring voices to join your song.
We desire to live in proximity to you, to be where your son
our Saviour Jesus is – so empower us to discern you in all
your ways, to witness to all, that they in turn may witness
your love for themselves, that this whole world would
witness in wonder and joy to the ways and means of your
redemption. For your glory we pray. Amen.

Notes

1 Walter Brueggemann, 1993, *Biblical Perspectives on Evangelism*, Nashville, TN: Abingdon Press, p. 45.

2 Dallas Willard, 1998, *The Divine Conspiracy*, London: Harper-Collins, p. 37.

3 Lesslie Newbigin, 2014, *The Gospel in a Pluralistic Society*, London: SPCK, p. 127.

4 Annie Dillard, 2011, *Pilgrim at Tinker Creek*, London: Canterbury Press, p. 123.

5 Dietrich Bonhoeffer, 1948 (2015), *Cost of Discipleship*, London: SCM Press, p. 6.

6 Andrew Root, 2017, *Faith Formation in a Secular Age*, Grand Rapids, MI: Baker Academic, p. 7.

7 Miroslav Volf and Matthew Croasmun, 2019, *For the Life of the World: Theology that Makes a Difference*, Grand Rapids, MI: Brazos Press, p. 55.

8 There are wonderful books on this theme; for example, John Inge, *A Christian Theology of Place* (London: Routledge & Kegan Paul, 2003) and particularly Andrew Rumsey, *Parish: An Anglican Theology of Place* (London: SCM Press, 2017).

9 Stefan Paas, 2016, *Church Planting in the Secular West*, Grand Rapids, MI: Eerdmans, chapter one.

10 Newbigin, *The Gospel in a Pluralistic Society*, p. 127.